Before the Kids and Mortgage

EYAL N. DANON

Before the Kids and Mortgage:
One Couple's Escape from the Ordinary
©2020, Eyal N. Danon

Publishing consultant: David Wogahn for AuthorImprints.com

*Dedicated to all the true wanderers
who transform everyday routines
into an adventure and a way of life.*

Not all those who wander are lost.

—J.R.R. Tolkien,
The Fellowship of The Ring

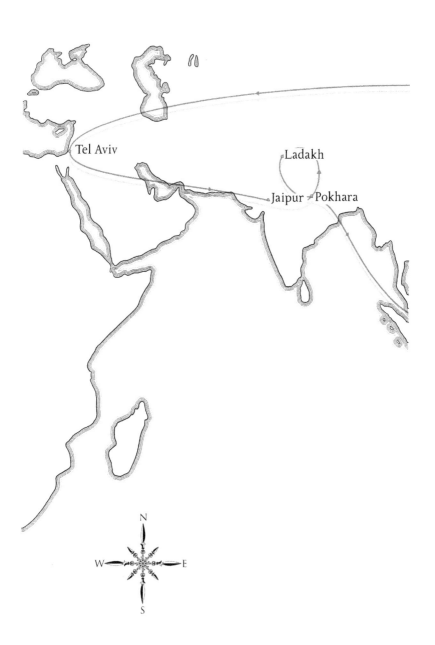

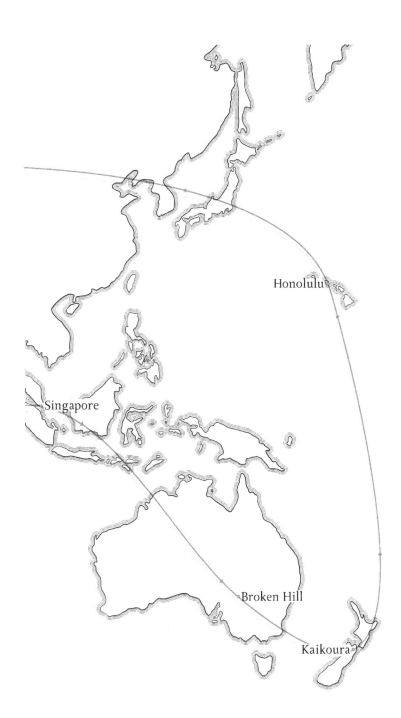

Singapore

Honolulu

Broken Hill

Kaikoura

CONTENTS

CHAPTER ONE

THE LOVE BOAT
ON THE KALI GANDAKI

IN A SMALL APARTMENT, THE telephone rings.

"Hello, I'm speaking with Eyal?" a man's voice asks in English with a heavy French accent.

"Yes," I reply. "Who is this?"

"This is Freddy, from the rafting trip in Nepal."

"Freddy! How are you? Is everything all right?"

"Yes, yes, everything is fine. Can you come fetch me?"

"What do you mean, 'fetch you'?" As far as I knew, Freddy was at that very moment in distant Brussels. "Where are you?"

"At your airport. I'm here, in Israel," Freddy explained patiently in his nasally voice. "Don't you remember? When we were in the Himalayas, I promised that if you two would get married, I'd come to your wedding."

Odelia, who was sitting beside me on the sofa, looked at me in wide-eyed astonishment. I hissed at her, "That nut got on a plane and is coming to our wedding!"

"Freddy," I yelled into the receiver, "Stay right where you are! We're coming to pick you up!"

❋ ❋ ❋

Our wedding was due to take place in a week's time, and we had a million loose ends to tie up. The last thing we needed was to have Freddy on our hands, this Belgian guy with whom we had spent all of one week in the wilds of Nepal, but his unexpected arrival was symbolic. Freddy's presence sparked memories of the first trip Odelia and I took together, to the Kali Gandaki River in the Himalayas, the place where it all began. Three months after Odelia and I started going together, we decided to travel to Nepal.

Odelia was frank about her motive for traveling. One of her closest girlfriends claimed that there was nothing like an adventure trip to discover whether the man you are seeing is truly compatible with you. "Taking an intense trip together reveals all your boyfriend's weak points," Odelia quoted her pal as saying, so I jumped at the opportunity.

"Well, then, let's travel to Nepal!" I had always dreamed of going to Nepal, the land of the lofty Himalayan Mountains, to follow in the footsteps of Edmund Hillary and Tenzing Norgay, the Sherpa. With this uncommon blend of interests, we took the first step on our Nepalese journey.

We agreed that this trip should be a thrilling adventure, the kind that comes along once in a lifetime, an unforgettable experience that would remain with us always. We decided on white-water rafting in the valleys of the Himalayas. Of all Nepal's impressive rivers, we opted for the Kali Gandaki, a river that runs through a nature reserve in the Annapurna mountain range, as the one that most suited our ambitions. Nearly every traveler to Nepal goes rafting there, on rivers with varying degrees of turbulence.

River running has an international grading system that rates the difficulty of rafting routes on a scale from one to six: a Class I is a calm little river with easy-flowing water, while a Class VI is "extreme" and "practically impossible" to navigate—Niagara Falls, for example.

The problem is that grading is not scientifically determined at all. It is based on an evaluation by a bunch of experienced river runners who show up at the river in question having equipped themselves with an impressive supply of bottled beer. They then proceed to hunker down, contemplating the rapids while tackling the beer, till they decide on the grade.

Even so, the novice traveler seeking a white-water experience in Nepal need not feel overwhelmed, as the likely choice comes down to one of two rivers: the Trisuli (Class III) or the Kali Gandaki (Class IV).

The Trisuli is known as the poor man's Kali Gandaki. It's essentially a calm, quiet river livened up by a few rapids that will barely interrupt a vacationer's peaceful relaxation. In contrast, the Kali Gandaki flows through the deepest river gorge on the planet. The many unpredictable stretches of white-water demand that river runners stay vigilant and keep up a concerted effort to remain on their rubber rafts. The difference between Class III and Class IV might as well be the difference between heaven and earth.

Odelia's inclination was clear: she preferred the Trisuli. She was afraid of the water and was not all that keen on the idea of rafting.

Hoping to prompt more enthusiasm, I redoubled my efforts to persuade her: "This is a once-in-a-lifetime opportunity. If you don't come along, you'll always regret having missed it." These were punctuated by assurances that the route was entirely safe. How I delivered all this in a convincing tone, heaven only knows, but Odelia finally agreed—with some qualms.

What neither of us realized, though, was that we were planning our ambitious trip right after monsoon season, when river rafting was most dangerous.

When you talk with experienced river runners about white-water rafting in the monsoon season, you will witness a strange phenomenon. Their eyes shine, their muscles tighten, their bodies tense, and a burst of vitality and raw energy floods them. They will make all sorts of complicated gesticulations with their hands, bobbing and weaving to represent the dreadful struggle with the waves. Their speech becomes a frenzied babble about "flow," "hydraulics," "maximum water quantity," and other professional terminology that the amateur rafter can only vaguely follow. We were in no way experienced rafters, nor could we imagine how the Kali Gandaki would look after the monsoons. And by the time we saw it, it was too late.

But first things first. At this stage in the journey, we were mere innocents who hadn't even gotten our feet wet. The buckles on our new backpacks sparkled with anticipation, our top-of-the-line hiking boots begged for the pristine trails, our shiny black raincoats were ready to handle any storm. Now the time had come to put our courage and equipment to the test.

Before boarding the raft, we had to choose our rafting guide, the individual into whose hands we would deliver our souls for the coming week. In Thamel, the main tourist center in the Nepalese capital, Katmandu, every travel agent was also a "certified" rafting guide who would take you—at a "special" rate, of course—on an unforgettable "once-in-a-lifetime" trip. Only the last part of that claim was accurate; you would be highly unlikely to forget a trip like this, should you survive it. This, however, the inexperienced traveler learns too late.

The question seemed to be whether to choose a local rafting outfit, or an established New Zealand-based rafting company, one that has an excellent reputation, modern equipment, professional guides, specially designed lifeboats, the possibility of airlift rescue, and gourmet fare. The local outfit, on the other hand, meant antiquated equipment without rescue arrangements. Meal service has two variations: indigenous or "European".

The Nepalese menu consisted of the ubiquitous *dal bhat*, a curried stew of lentils and rice. The European menu featured several weird variations on porridge— basically a cold, nondescript glop with scant resemblance to the classic British breakfast staple.

The New Zealand–based company charged $150 for a five-day rafting trip; the Nepalese outfit, with humble gratitude, would accept all of $50, a mere third of its competitor's fee. Like most of our cohorts we had limited funds, so every expense ultimately meant heading home that much earlier. With that decision out of the way, we found ourselves on a rickety bus headed for Naya Pul, the source of the Kali Gandaki.

It was on the way to Naya Pul that our group formed, the chosen comrades with whom we would board a little rubber raft for the better part of a week. Netta, an accountant from Tel Aviv, and Michael from Alaska (whom we referred to privately as Klondike Mike), we'd already met in the legendary Pumpernickel restaurant back in Katmandu.

Michael was a tall, muscular fellow of about twenty-five who exuded energy and enthusiasm on this, his first trip outside his native Alaska. His appearance was a startling juxtaposition of massive physical strength and innocent blue eyes shining from a baby face. Michael's dream was to conquer Mount Everest. Before setting forth on his journey to the East, he had racked up experience by making lengthy solo treks through the most remote parts of Alaska. Equipped with a tent and sleeping bag good for temperatures down to −18°F, plus cutting-edge climbing gear for which he spared no expense, Michael would scale a glacier, reach its promontory, then set up camp to spend a few days there.

We instantly appreciated the latent potential of this rugged specimen. Somebody would have to paddle the raft, after all, so what could be better than giving Michael the opportunity to limber up en route to Everest? During the lively bus ride to Naya Pul, we discovered that among this company of forty wannabe river rats, thirty of us held Israeli citizenship. We took an unofficial census of the others. Michael was already seated with us, basking in the glow of admiring glances from the female passengers. The seven Japanese travelers were engaged in an animated discussion at the front of the bus, oblivious to the rest of us. That left two remaining strangers: Freddy the Belgian and a New Zealander named Dean, who were seated side by side at the back of the bus, observing the gregarious mob.

In the distance, we could glimpse brief flashes of the turbulent river with its muddy froth. It resembled an ominous cross between an earthquake and a flash flood. The water was a dismal shade of grey spotted with ugly whirlpools of liquid mud. The river growled in threatening tones like a gangster who was not getting his protection money. The torrent rushed with surging force over boulders that appeared to have been strewn randomly in its path. The Kali Gandaki was revealing its raw, untamed nature.

In a burst of anxiety, we were motivated to adopt the two strangers into our group. There was a fair likelihood that they would be more reliable than a bunch of Israelis with their characteristic attitude of *"Ahhh, c'mon, trust me!"* What we needed to survive the expedition, we told ourselves, was a foreign legion, skilled and responsible. Odelia and I plotted our moves: I would approach the Belgian and she would work her wiles on the New Zealander.

I studied my target, contemplating my opening gambit. He appeared to be in his early twenties: lean, bespectacled, with a wispy mane of hair and a few days' growth of whiskers. In contrast to the gaggle of Israelis, who sported a clashing array of multicolored tops with wide-legged, unisex harem pants, he wore a pair of jeans with a clean white shirt tucked firmly into his waistband. Racking my brain for Belgian material, all I could come up with was Jean-Claude Van Damme. Not much of a conversation starter, I feared, but it would have to do. As I made my way over to Freddy's seat, he looked up in wonder at what I might have in mind. The directness of his gaze unsettled me.

"Umm, maybe you know Jean-Claude Van Damme?" I murmured.

"Sure, I've heard of him," my Belgian replied with an engaging smile, "but he's not much of a Belgian anymore, having spent such a long time in Hollywood."

Thus, we launched our first conversation, during which Freddy revealed himself to be a charming fellow with a dull job as a computer engineer at IBM's main offices in Brussels, who had managed, despite the demands of his day job, to travel all over the world. Even better: not only did he agree to join our group, he undertook to include the introverted Dean, who meanwhile had dozed off beside him.

We alighted from the bus at the rafting departure point. From there, our field of vision was limited by the river's sharp swerve to the right; all we could see was a calm stretch of flowing water.

Our guide commenced handing out the lifesaving equipment, and there began to appear the first cracks in the brave facade we had all been keeping up. The life vests seemed to be faded relics of a glorious past. They were of a nondescript, greenish-pinkish color, perforated with an assortment of rips and tears, not all of which had been repaired with makeshift patches. The buckles on the life vests did not connect with a decisive, confidence-inspiring click, but slid around our bodies as though they had a life of their own. For headgear, we were given helmets made of flimsy red plastic. They reminded us of the kind kids wear when playing fireman in the backyard: far too large to be of any practical use. When tied securely under the chin, their grubby strings proved more effective as a strangulation device.

Each of us was then given a paddle made of cheap plastic that already showed cracks. As for the rafts that would be our sole mode of transportation, these turned out to be nothing more than inflatable rubber rafts. Despite their numerous visible patches, such a quantity of holes remained that it would be necessary to stop every few hours to pump air into the rafts. The perpetual whistle of air escaping from their hidden holes was a subject of amusement—until, that is, we went out on the river.

We gathered for an explanatory lecture on what we could soon expect. The head Nepalese guide was a muscular guy in a long tank top—an authentic Israeli army undershirt received from a grateful survivor of a previous expedition. He leapt onto one of the rafts in an athletic move, grabbed a paddle, and began speaking in broken English spiced with Hebrew and Nepali words:

"OK, YOU LISTEN, NO BALAGAN,* SHANTI,** TAKE PADDLE, NO WORRY!"

He rushed into a rapid sequence of instructions we failed to grasp. We consoled ourselves with the thought that our own guide would patiently explain everything

---

* Hebrew slang: disorder, mess, utter chaos
** Contemporary Hebrew: the essence of Eastern mystical serenity, peace and love.

to us. Indeed, a few moments before we were to enter the river, our guide showed up. Deepak was a tough Nepalese kid with a thin, muscular body, a thick mop of frizzy hair, and a wild look in his eyes. The total repertoire of Deepak's English vocabulary consisted of the brief phrase "FORWARD TOGETHER," shouted at frequent intervals, interspersed on rare occasions with "ONLY LEFT" and "ONLY RIGHT." The rest of his messages were delivered by means of intense glares, especially when someone was not performing as required. He would then resort to assorted hand gestures and violent facial expressions accompanied by juicy curses in throaty Nepali. When we asked the head guide how old Deepak was, we discovered he was all of fifteen.

It was late in the afternoon when we boarded our raft to set out on the river. A chilly wind had begun to blow across the surface of the Kali Gandaki, prompting us Hebrew speakers to spontaneously rechristen it the Kar Li ("I'm cold") Gandaki. With the source of Nepal's rivers up among the mighty peaks of the Himalayan range, the water temperature did not let us forget our geography for a moment.

The seating arrangement on the raft, it turned out, was of utmost significance. Those paddling up front bore the brunt of the waves. The middle seats were safest, the rear position meant asking for trouble. Michael leaped forward and settled himself at the prow; Freddy, in a bold move, sat down beside him. Odelia and Netta snuggled

into the center, leaving me and our New Zealander stationed at the rear. Our faithful guide Deepak positioned
himself at the very back of the raft like an Oriental
prince. He gripped a massive hunk of wood that appeared
to be an entire tree trunk, intending to use it as a primitive rudder for adjusting our course through the rapids. Altogether, we were in high spirits. We were about to
spend five days on this exciting river. Our expectations
and enthusiasm were contagious.

Right away we discovered that the Nepalese rafting
company was of the shock-treatment school when it came
to acquainting novices with the river. Barely five minutes
after we boarded the rafts, we began to hear a threatening
roar from afar. In that interval, Deepak did his best to
instill within us a sense of teamwork while imparting his
version of River Rafting 101: how to handle a paddle and
how to work in coordination with each other. The initial
glow of euphoria dissipated; a chilly feeling of anxiety
enveloped us. Truth be told, all of us (apart from Michael)
were edging toward panic.

I was concerned for Odelia, as she was afraid of drown-
ing. Every time she'd talked about this possibility, she'd
shivered in terror and I'd hurried to reassure her in a
confident tone. "What will happen if you fall in?" I would
say, shrugging my shoulders. "I'd get you out of the water.
You have nothing to worry about." I now realized that if
she were to fall into the rapids, I would be helpless to help
her. Sunk deep in these thoughts, I left off paddling for a

moment. I was roused by a hoarse scream from the stern of the raft: Deepak was cursing me in guttural Nepali, winding up with the ultimate: "LAZY ITALIAN!" This, we were to learn, was reserved for the toughest cases. What the original Italian had done to deserve this vast contempt from Deepak, we would never know. For the duration of our journey we tried to avoid whatever would provoke this alarming phrase.

Approaching the first set of rapids at a frightening pace, we were a confused, oddly matched crew that had no clue what we'd signed up for. As the din of the rushing water intensified, we gripped our paddles all the harder. Our chatter ceased. I touched Odelia's shoulder and she turned toward me slowly. Her lips were pale and stretched thin; her eyes darted from side to side. I tried to say something, but no words came out. I swallowed hard, praying that this would turn out well.

Deepak, a master of timing, chose this point to burst into what sounded like a Nepalese river chantey. The simple lyrics washed over us soothingly like the flowing river. Here they are, reproduced to the best of my recollection:

Rasampi-ri-ri
Rasampi-ri-ri
Urrah jaooki
Dadema bangen
Rasampi-ri-riiiiiiiiii

I looked around me at the members of our plucky squad. They all appeared terrified. The greenish life vests and red helmets were the perfect accessories to accent the pale, blanched faces of my comrades in adventure, whose whitened knuckles betrayed an excessively hard grip on the paddles. Only Michael remained calm as he sang the catchy Nepalese tune with juvenile enthusiasm, distorting the foreign syllables, horrendously off-key.

We had a clear view of what awaited us. The river was bisected by a series of giant boulders that made its turbulent waters surge and roil in a powerful flood. With a sense of terrible fear, I turned to Odelia and was somewhat relieved to see that she had abandoned paddling and was crouching at the bottom of the raft, clinging tightly to a rope that tied our equipment.

Deepak steered the raft into the current. His voice rose above the din of the rushing waters. "FORWARD TOGETHER!" came his battle cry—and before there was time to think, we were amid the tumultuous, thrashing torrent. It was at this point that we caught sight of Freddy flying high through the air, arms flung wide, his face a dreadful mix of astonishment and fear.

It was impossible to come to his aid. Giant mud waves washed over the raft and we were fighting for our lives, paddles in the air. All I could see was Michael's broad back as he battled the waves, fighting for us all. It would be no exaggeration to say that at this point, I simply loved the guy.

The raft rocked amid colossal waves. We were in the middle of the rapids, surrounded by mud-brown water that swirled around huge boulders. We managed to avoid one giant rock, but the whirlpool alongside it pulled our puny raft into its vortex and spun us around. Deepak struck the boulder with his paddle, freeing us from the whirlpool. We lurched forward.

The waves competed in a show of strength. After what seemed like an eternity, we reached the end of the rapids. Our raft was full of water, we were soaked through—but we had done it! Odelia was stark white, breathing with difficulty. The others roared with delight, giddily releasing their pent-up tensions.

Michael asked, "Where's Freddy?"

We looked around. The other rafts went by; poor Freddy was not on any of them. Deepak, steering between the other rafts, commanded us to row quickly forward. After five minutes of strenuous paddling, we were rewarded by the sight of Freddy: clinging to a boulder at the river's edge, clutching his paddle with his left hand. He appeared dazed, like a kitten that had fallen into the water, his wet, matted hair framing his pale face. Though his entire body was shuddering with chills, he was in one piece.

We lifted our companion onto our raft, whereupon he took his seat up front and began paddling. Other than the sound of his teeth chattering, we didn't hear anything from him. He was the picture of grim determination as he focused on his strokes. He didn't stop even when we reached a calm stretch, paddling as if he was trying to get somewhere important. Only when evening fell and we were securely anchored for the night did Freddy release his tight grip on his paddle.

All through that evening, he remained mute. The next morning, he began to talk—but none of us could understand a word of what he said. Freddy was speaking in French. At first we thought he was kidding around, but after a few minutes we realized that he had somehow forgotten his English. None of us knew any French, so all we could do was shake our heads at him while trying to keep a straight face. After several hours, much to everyone's relief, he resumed speaking English. Everyone avoided mentioning the spell of French, and Freddy never made further reference to his airborne episode and its waterlogged aftermath.

The journey progressed as planned. We would paddle onward from morning till sometime in the afternoon, then reach our destination, set up our campsite, and relax for the rest of the evening. The rapids were not so scary as our panic level dropped, and we began to get acquainted with travelers from other rafts. The Japanese contingent remained aloof, though; they paddled in unison, ate separately from the rest of their companions, and set up camp according to a precise plan.

The rest of us river runners found ourselves forming a cohesive group. Each evening we sat for hours around the campfire sharing tall tales, getting to know one another.

The bonds of camaraderie began to develop among us: Michael and Netta were spotted strolling along the riverbank, and there were signs of a budding romance between our tough teenaged guide, Deepak, and Adi, a pretty Israeli girl.

Although Freddy and Dean would sit down with us, Dean never took an active part in the conversation. Freddy would go on in detail, telling Odelia and me about his life in Belgium. To our surprise, he revealed considerable curiosity about life in Israel. "Come see for yourself," we told him one evening, to which he nodded in his earnest manner.

"When you two get married, let me know, I'll be there."

We laughed. We had not even begun to think about returning home to Israel, let alone planning a wedding.

After several days, the river changed character and became placid. It was possible to drift along without any effort, paddles raised, simply letting the sun warm our bodies while the current carried us forward.

One evening, the Nepalese guides lit an extra-large bonfire and gathered us all for a talk. It was a gorgeous evening. We sat on the riverbank under innumerable stars that were visible far above the canyon's tall walls. The chief guide, paddle in hand, began to speak. He referred first to the rapid where Freddy had been launched aloft from our raft. That one, he said, was known as Little Brother. Everyone cheered, backslapping and sharing war stories of how they survived the rapid.

After we calmed down, the guide continued. "Tomorrow we'll be rafting through Big Brother." He paused to make sure we understood, then nodded, opened his hands wide, and said,

"Big Brother is big trouble."

Only Michael laughed.

The guide then described the best way to attack the rapid. We did not understand most of what he was talking about, but his tone and expression spoke volumes. We managed to comprehend that in the middle of the rapid we'd go over a waterfall with a drop of fifteen feet. While descending this waterfall, we were supposed to raise our paddles and hold them upright to avoid hitting our fellow rafters on the head.

Odelia turned to me and said firmly,

"I have no intention of going through Big Brother. Little Brother was enough."

"So what will you do?" I asked. "That's the only way to continue with our trip down the river."

"I don't care. I'm ready to climb the canyon walls, if that's what it takes, and hike till we get to some village."

I scanned the sheer face of the canyon walls. It would be easier to sprout wings and fly over them than to scale them. Besides, we were out in the middle of nowhere. I remembered the prophetic advice of Odelia's girlfriend, that this trip would test the bond between us, and my feeling of helplessness increased.

In the morning, we mounted the raft in silence under grey skies and a cold wind.

"We'll cross that rapid when we come to it," I finally muttered. Odelia shook her head no.

After an hour of paddling, we approached the last calm stretch of the river. Deepak pointed out a large, flat expanse of exposed boulder, a vantage point for assessing the rapids ahead. With a huge sense of relief, I heard him say that anyone who had any hesitations could get around Big Brother by walking along the riverbank. I looked over at Odelia; the color was returning to her cheeks. In a matter of minutes, she had gathered around her all the other rafters who preferred to experience the rafts' descent vicariously, as spectators from the shore.

We sat on the flat stone looking at a series of steep waterfalls. The head guide pointed out the best route across the rapids, but the noise was so deafening that we could not follow what he said. The rapids were wide at the outset, ending in a massive waterfall between narrow rock walls. This time we knew what we were getting into and had no expectations of the sort of euphoric cheer with which we had greeted Little Brother.

Somehow the guides in their infinite wisdom decided that our raft would be the first to go through. We were ready for adventure. In a state of anticipation, I stared at the rocks ahead through narrowed eyes.

The head guide looked our way, then bellowed something in Nepali.

Deepak replied, then turned to us. "LISTEN, NO SCARED, TOGETHER NOW!"

With this, Deepak gave a forceful shove that launched the raft toward the rapids, and adrenaline rushed through my veins like the current sweeping us forward. Freddy was tense, with grim determination in his eyes. Michael was cinching his life vest like a battle-seasoned soldier. No one was smiling. I waved at Odelia over on the shore, and she waved back at me.

Before we knew it, we were amid the rapids.

We floated atop a buoyant current that led directly to the drop-off point. Deepak attempted to rotate the raft so we could see what awaited us, but it was too late. Gigantic muddy waves washed over us, soaking us from head to toe. As we reached the brink of the waterfall, he thundered, "PADDLE IN AIR!"

The little raft wobbled; we were suspended in midair, then made a sudden, steep drop at great speed. I held my breath as our raft plummeted toward the stormy abyss below. Everything whirled around me as I tried desperately to maintain my balance.

Within a few seconds, it was over. Odelia's team cheered us on from the rocky shoreline; I could make her out among them. Despite my fondest desire to share this experience with her, at that moment I understood that sometimes we would have to take different paths to get to our mutual destination. I hoped that I would be able to be more flexible in similar situations in the future.

At the end of our journey, we parted from our raft-mates with hugs, promising to stay in touch. Even Dean, the taciturn, blasé New Zealander who had never called any of us by name during the intense week we shared on the river, was moved by our emotional parting.

Several months later, Odelia and I were back home in Israel. By then we understood that having gone through the Kali Gandaki in one piece, we could make it through anything together—so we decided to get married. Invitations were sent to everyone we knew, including our traveling companions from our Nepal trip. Freddy replied with a letter of congratulations. He wrote how excited he was for us and shared his intent to come to the wedding, as promised. We didn't pay much attention until he called to tell us he was waiting at the airport.

When we sighted him at Ben Gurion Airport in Israel, he looked quite festive, if rather sticky with perspiration, embalmed in a three-piece suit. He looked different from our rafting days. We wondered how much we knew him.

During the week he spent at our house, Freddy was calm and relaxed. Not for a moment did he reveal the tremendous potential that lay within him. This we were to discover after the conclusion of the wedding ceremony. Once the canopy was out of the way, he began to warm up. When the musicians picked up the tempo, Freddy began to shed his clothes, and before our astonished eyes he transformed into Belgium's answer to John Travolta. With a skilled motion he rid himself of his necktie, then a few minutes later his suit jacket. This he flung with a flip of the wrist, sending it sailing over the crowd of dazzled females who gazed at him with growing appreciation. His vest was next to go. Now Freddie was dancing like a madman, executing a bizarre series of leaps. Several of the older guests were convinced that he was part of the scheduled entertainment, a male stripper brought in from Europe.

One disco hit followed another and Freddy kept up the pace. By now a crowd had formed around him, clapping fervently with the rhythm. Were we seeing our Freddy in his native element? Or had the rafting incident been so traumatic that it drove him mad?

Rivers of perspiration soaked his shirt, his shoulders rose and fell, his hips gyrated to some inner rhythm of their own. He was caught up in total ecstasy as we looked on in fascination. At some point, our beautiful friend Maya volunteered as his dance partner. On they danced until the party ended, and it was only a matter of months before Maya moved to Brussels to live with him.

What about us, you may ask? Well, we were on our way again. Once bitten by the travel bug, we couldn't resist the taste of freedom. Although everything seemed calm and life was flowing along smoothly, it wasn't long before I decided to convince Odelia that we should take another trip together, a more ambitious adventure than the first.

I wanted to leave everything behind, travel to faraway lands, someplace where we could be free of alarm clocks, the daily news, obligations to fulfill. I dreamed of a leisurely, unstructured trip to the Far East, a journey on which we'd be able to decide on the spur of the moment to stop at any spot that appealed to us, or to cross a border for another adventure.

Odelia was not sure such a long trip was a good idea. "Both of us are over thirty years old," she said. "Don't you think it's time for us to act our age, take out a mortgage, become parents? It's time we start thinking of ourselves as a family, not as a couple," she asserted with healthy logic. "Besides, we've already traveled to the Far East. We could always go back with the kids."

This was a wise, reasoned contention, but I couldn't give up on my dream. Once Odelia understood this, she came around. We decided to embark on this adventure. Having gotten the required series of inoculations, we booked a flight to Nepal and acquired some new gear, including a giant map of the world. After an emotional leave-taking from family and friends, we boarded a flight to New Delhi with a connection to Katmandu, Nepal.

As the plane took off, we settled into our seats. We had done everything we could to prepare for this journey, sold everything we possessed, said our goodbyes to whomever mattered. The time had come to start a new chapter in our lives—and we realized with a rush of expectations and emotions that the adventure we had been longing for was about to begin.

CHAPTER TWO

MICHAEL THE BOSS

A YEAR PASSED, AND WE found ourselves again in the picturesque town of Pokhara in Nepal, the starting point for traveling in the Himalayas. Here, we determined, where we had experienced our unforgettable rafting adventure, would be an appropriate beginning for the big journey.

This time around we decided to take our time, not rush anywhere, see where the path would take us. We strolled along the busy, uncared-for main street, looking for a decent place to rest awhile and enjoy the carefree ambience of this charming town. An hour later we found a delightful corner: a groomed hotel with the pretentious name of Alpine Villa.

The hotel was surrounded by a beautiful garden with colorful flower beds, furnishings made of straw, and swaying palm trees. The guest rooms were full of light. A devoted Nepalese crew was working everywhere, painting, pruning, and cleaning. None of the workers spoke English, and whoever we addressed repeated the name "Michael" as if it were a spell. One after the other, the devoted workers mumbled this name while waving up their hands, as if to say that Michael's spirit was everywhere but nowhere in particular. We had almost given up on finding the mysterious guy when he showed up behind us, patting my back and smiling, revealing a mouthful of big white teeth.

Michael was tall and sturdy, with a mane brushed backward, sort of John-Travolta style. He was wearing a Diadora tracksuit and huge tinted golden Ray-Ban glasses. He had a million-dollar smile backed up by the charisma of a Bollywood star.

Michael told us he had purchased the place the week before, and that we were his first guests. His English was perfect. Most of the hostel managers in the East spoke poor English and used their children, who studied English at school, to explain themselves. When we asked him how much the pleasure of staying in his lovely hotel would cost us, Michael surprised us when he said with a charming smile, "One hundred rupees, including breakfast."

The place was worth much more, but we assumed the rate was an introductory promotional rate for the new hotel. A few minutes after we entered our room, two glasses of papaya juice decorated with orange slices showed up. "It's on the house, from Michael," mumbled the young Nepalese worker.

We were sure that after such a start we should expect a dream vacation. After a sweet siesta, Odelia was freshening up in the shower, whistling a jolly song that was cut off when the shower head flopped onto her head with a metallic sound. I tried to attach it back, but the shower head refused to reconnect to the hose.

"That's how it is in a running-in period," I tried to assure her. "One may expect such minor failures."

After a delicious dinner at an Indian restaurant facing the lake, we returned to our room and fell asleep on the huge bed. In the middle of the night, the bed frame broke down with a sickening screech and fell to the green rug, taking a mighty blow. With a slight limp, I stepped out of the room to let the staff know of the incident. The hotel was dark, shut down like a Sicilian widow. I found one of the employees watching TV at the reception desk and explained with hand gestures what had happened. He nodded; his expression seemed to convey that this development was typical.

Five minutes later Michael himself arrived in our room wearing boxer underwear from the time of Muhammad Ali, holding a big stone he had most likely found in the garden. He attacked the poor bed, beating it mercilessly until he managed to get the broken boards back into shape.

Over the next few days, we learned that Michael did not consider himself a typical Nepalese. He claimed to be an American citizen, different from his ragtag crew of Indian-Nepalese employees. We never saw his American passport, so the only relic that proved his ties to the

United States was the worn-out grey jacket he wore every evening. Michael told us that the jacket was sewed for him in New York by Jack Nicholson's personal tailor.

In the evening when the sun painted the magnificent Phewa Lake red, Michael came to the office all shaved and perfumed, his mane combed back fashionably, a contented smile on his face. Then he would take his famous jacket out of the closet, brush it with a special brush, and put it on carefully. Afterwards, he would walk around his kingdom like a peacock, bossing around his employees like a king descending for a stroll among his primitive subordinates.

Michael displayed more Western elements: smoking thick cigars, drinking choice whiskeys, gambling in a luxurious Katmandu casino, viewing the *Godfather* movies obsessively. His employees feared and admired him; they regarded him as a successful businessman who was able to thrive in the United States against all odds.

It was disorienting to watch him try to pull off this American persona, but his saving grace was his bountiful natural charisma that effortlessly bridged the gap between myth and reality. Our encounters provided me with abundant opportunities to test my theory that highly confident people create their own future, regardless of their real talents.

Michael was so eager to prove himself a man of the world that he never admitted ignorance in any field; he repeated "I know that" with alarming frequency. If someone had told him the world was rectangular, I am sure he would have smiled brightly and repeated the phrase in his deep baritone: "I know that." He said the words with the confidence of someone who *knew*, and it was difficult not to believe him.

Michael had another interesting habit of trying to connect every topic to his own background. For example, when German guests came to the hotel, he tried to impress them by stammering in barely intelligible German. When the astonished guests asked him where he picked up such a vocabulary, he smiled and said that his wife was a German who belonged to an aristocratic family from Frankfurt.

One evening when we were talking about Judaism, Michael surprised us with news that cemented his greatness forever.

"To tell you the truth," he said, combing back his slicked hair with his hand, "my mother is Jewish."

After that, we were like brothers of the same faith. We sat in his tiny office for lengthy evenings drinking whiskey over ice and watching the *Godfather* movies. Michael was enchanted by the Corleone family in New York, reciting lines from all three pictures. His favorite scene was when Michael Corleone visits his father in the hospital after the old don is critically injured in a botched hit. Up to this point in the movie, Michael Corleone has been reluctant to enter the family business.

To his surprise, Michael Corleone finds out that the guards assigned to his unconscious father have disappeared. The next hit attempt is imminent. Michael moves him to another room, then goes to the lobby to prevent the hit men from entering the hospital. At the entrance he bumps into Enzo the baker, an old friend of his father, who shows up with a bouquet of flowers. Enzo is far from the ideal partner to protect Don Corleone, but in a brilliant move, Michael stations himself with Enzo outside the hospital so the hit men will believe his father is protected.

Menacing music begins. A long car moves toward the entrance. Poor Enzo knows he is in harm's way. Michael raises his collar; Enzo does the same. The car inches forward, its passengers examining Michael and Enzo for a long spell that seems like eternity before the car pulls away. The danger is over. Enzo tries to light a cigarette to calm his nerves, but his hands are too shaky. Michael lights it for him. He looks at his hand and realizes that the event did not affect him. He managed to save his father, and he understands that he is cut out for the mafia business after all.

Each time we saw this scene, Michael the Boss watched with great focus. The first time we watched it together, he stopped the video at the end of this scene and addressed me.

"Do you see what I see?"

I nodded.

"He didn't just save his father. He did much more than that," Michael said in his deep voice. He rose from his chair, pacing the small office, tapping his shoulder several times to contain his excitement. Then he turned to me and said, "He managed to face his moment of truth and come out the other side. That means that he is a man that can determine his own fate."

I thought about this. Even though Michael the Boss was a con man with unrealistic fantasies, there was a grain of truth in his words. My father had an interesting theory on why so few people are successful in life. According to him, every person on this planet is given at least three chances to succeed, regardless of their status or position. He called these opportunities the "success train." The train is always moving, but it's only at certain moments that we can make a run for it and jump aboard. He then added—with his finger raised for emphasis—that the vast majority of people, 99% of anyone you will come in contact with, will not be able to recognize that the success train is out there, right now, calling their name, urging them to make the jump. My father explained that most people are too busy working, making a living, paying the bills, making ends meet; that they don't bother to take a breather and recognize with fresh eyes the opportunities that life presents to each one of us.

I was mesmerized by this story of the success train, especially the final twist: that only one percent of people *can* see one of the three major opportunities coming their

way. He explained that while these individuals could recognize the opportunities in front of them, only a tiny
portion of that one percent would drop everything and
jump on the train. That really piqued my interest as a kid.
Why on earth would someone miss out on such a grand,
rare opportunity, I wondered to myself. If you can see the
train coming and you know that it could lead you to your
dream destination, why wouldn't you jump on it?

Michael the Boss was a talented, persuasive storyteller.
He could talk about any subject with passion and confidence. His selection of stories was amazing, and oftentimes I would be captivated by his charm, getting caught
up in the yarns he was spinning. One of the stories he
told repeatedly was a tall tale about his family's fortune
in the Maldives islands. He claimed that his family owned
a few islands in the Indian Ocean, where they established
a hotel chain of the highest standard. Michael elaborated
about the unique look of the hotels and shared with me a
tattered brochure featuring a stunning hotel overlooking
a beautiful lagoon. How all that wealth settled in with
the five-bucks-a-night hostel he was managing in Nepal,
I would never know.

After several weeks and a few whiskey bottles, Michael
claimed to have been involved in developing a cure for
cancer in cooperation with an American scientist.

"A cure made of mysterious ingredients," he said in
his deep, baritone voice. They were, he said, on the verge
of a breakthrough that would make him and his partner

obscenely wealthy. At this point, Michael would lower his voice and look around furtively, although we were alone in his closed office in far-off Nepal.

"There are certain people that are not interested in seeing us developing the serum," he whispered. "They would kill me if they found out how close we are to finding a cure."

I glanced at the window, worried that a black car with armed men would pop up out of the darkness to take Michael away. The black car never showed up, though, and we had the privilege of hearing more brilliant stories from this unexpected person.

Michael admired everything related to the United States. In the first days of our friendship, I told him I'd been working in hotel management, but did not mention any other details. One evening, my hotel career came up, and the change in Michael was astonishing. His eyes shone and he straightened up in his chair, wishing to know more details. Eventually I went to my room and fetched a brochure of a luxurious Miami hotel where I used to work, part of an exclusive members-only club. I carried the brochure with me as sort of a naïve insurance policy in case our money would dry up and I would need to get a job at a hotel.

Michael grabbed the brochure. He held the fancy chromo paper with awe, his eyes caressing the high-quality color photos, scanning the private golf course, swallowing the yachts docked in the marina, the close-up photos of the lobby. He was mesmerized, flipping the pages back and forth like a kid who received a precious gift for Christmas. When he got to the photos of the rooms, he found his pièce-de-résistance, the image that settled the case: a photo of a bathroom in one of the guest rooms. His mouth opened as if searching for words, but for the first time since I'd met him, he was silent. The bathroom in the picture was laced with Italian marble and conveyed pampering comfort: thick robes, fluffy towels, an abundance of beauty products on the vanity like royal guards protecting a king. But what charmed Michael most, what stopped his fluent and constant chatter, was the state-of-the-art television stationed high above the sink, embedded in the mirror.

"Imagine," he mumbled after a while. "A television in the bathroom."

This was irrefutable proof of America's greatness, of its enormous richness and abundance. He turned to me, his eyes shining.

"Tell me, it's in one unique suite, isn't it?"

"No," I answered with deliberate nonchalance. "Every room has a television in the bathroom."

"You mean, in the luxurious rooms, those kept for serious businessmen?"

I restated my words. He looked down, then straightened up and said in his deep voice, "But this must be the only television in the room."

I broke the news to him that there was another wide-screen television in every room.

With his head bowed slightly, Michael asked what the nightly rate was. When I answered, his shoulders slumped and he leaned a bit toward me. His breath smelt of alcohol and tickled my nostrils when he whispered, "How long did you work there?"

"Six years," I answered.

"And you studied in the United States as well?"

"I have both my degrees from American universities."

This was the turning point in our relationship. Up to that point Michael had regarded Odelia and me as a nice couple, inexperienced backpackers to whom one could tell all kinds of grand stories without worrying too much about accuracy. From that moment on, his attitude changed. On the spot, my role was upgraded: from a drinking and storytelling companion to a close business adviser.

The next day, Michael told us that we would stay in the hotel for free, in any room we chose, for as long as we desired. He transferred us to the most luxurious room he had, spacious and full of light, with two broad, comfortable beds and a bathroom with flowing hot water. Plants covered the large windows, creating the impression of an enchanted hanging garden. The view was wonderful. Through one of the windows we could see the amazing Annapurna mountains, and on a nice day, the holy Machapuchare peak. We could not believe our luck! Such a room with such a view would have cost us a month's salary anywhere else in the world, yet here we got it for free! The sun shone through the plants and created a colorful mosaic in the room. Odelia and I smiled at each other like kids who'd won a big prize at the carnival.

The initial task given to me was to review all aspects of the hotel's operation and come up with easy-to-implement solutions. There were some issues that needed immediate attention, and Michael accepted every bit of advice I gave him. He was an excellent organizer, and his crew followed his orders without question or doubt, so in a short time I was able to change anything I disliked, with no restrictions. With Michael, there was no gap between an idea and its immediate implementation. Anything I suggested was carried out right away without objections or arguments.

My first recommendation was about paint; the hotel's exterior was pale and unattractive. When I mentioned to Michael that the hotel needed a new coat of paint, he nodded and said nothing. The next morning over breakfast, he asked offhandedly what my favorite color was, and I replied that it was blue. He nodded, then moved on to one of his favorite topics, the alleged fortune his family had accumulated in the Maldives. An hour later, Odelia and I left to spend the day at the lake. To our surprise, when we returned in the evening, we could not find our hotel. We wandered through the streets for a while, blinded by the orange sunset, before it dawned on us that the monstrosity painted in psychedelic blue past which we had walked several times was our beloved Alpine Villa hotel.

After that experience, I should have been more careful with my recommendations, but things did not go that way. Michael and I planned a fancy restaurant with a huge straw roof, bamboo chairs, and special lighting that made it look like a tropical island. We created an international menu with an eye toward classical European dishes, transformed the hotel's entrance, wrote a new brochure, and added new flowerpots and hammocks. In a redemptive move, the horrific blue walls were painted over with soothing pastels.

I gave the employees a brief training in quality service, and Odelia taught them key phrases in English. After an intensive week they all knew how to say "no problem." The diligent ones could add "problem solved" while smiling and nodding their heads.

I began to understand how the Indian maharajas had lived. One word from me was enough to change the atmosphere. It was a surreal experience. But things were not always executed to my satisfaction. The impressive palm tree I wished to trim a bit was ruthlessly cut off. The new intimate lighting I had planned became dreadful projectors that scanned the horizon in constant motion, transforming the romantic ambience I had hoped for into a fortified prison.

In the meantime, the employees started to evade me. Whenever I came up with a new way to improve the hotel or the customer experience, there were fewer and fewer workers to be found. Eventually I had to deliver the ideas to Michael himself, who still trusted my advice.

Although Odelia and I lived like royalty at the Alpine Villa, our next destination was Rajasthan in India. We both desired to get to know the smells, sounds, and sights of exotic India. I knew that saying farewell to Michael would not be easy, so I postponed the conversation. When the day came that I had to let him know about our coming departure, it happened during the daily drinking ceremony. As usual, we watched *The Godfather*. Enzo tried to light a cigarette with a shaky hand, and Michael Corleone helped him with a steady hand. When the cigarette was lit, I looked at Michael and told him it was time for me to look for my own moment of truth, in the big wide world that lived and breathed outside of Alpine Villa in Pokhara, Nepal.

"We are planning to leave by the end of the week," I announced. "We want to move on with our trip. It's important to us to continue our journey."

He smiled approvingly, touching his chin with his left hand while nodding like an astute sage, as if he'd seen this move from a mile away. I waited with bated breath, and then he said, smiling and nodding, "I know that."

CHAPTER THREE

DAUGHTERS, DAUGHTERS

INDIA WAS OUR NEXT STOP. Like all travelers to the East, we'd heard that India was amazing, and that one must spend quite a long time there to absorb its hidden beauty. We'd also gathered that India offered an unceasing attack on the senses, and that the initial adjustment would not be easy, but that did not dampen our enthusiasm. India with all its wonders awaited us just a one-hour flight from Katmandu.

Who could imagine that for all its wonders, a simple rickshaw driver from Jaipur, the desert-like capital of Rajasthan, would leave such an unforgettable imprint on us?

Indian rickshaw drivers represent what writers and intellectuals like to call "the real India," perhaps because of their colorful outfits or their legendary driving ability. Or maybe because they are present everywhere, ignoring the cold winter winds, the monsoon rain, the fervent heat, waiting for the random backpacker whose payment for a single ride might provide a week's living for an entire family.

When an innocent traveler arrives at a bus or train station in India, a mass of drivers swarm around her. Each driver's dream is to catch an inexperienced backpacker and sell her as much as he can—hotel accommodations, city tour rides, meals, shopping—an endless list. To perform this complicated and sensitive task, a rickshaw driver must acquire the backpacker's trust before getting her to ride in his rickshaw. To trap you in his net, a good rickshaw driver will agree to take you anywhere you like for a ridiculous price. He knows that this way he will most likely own you for the rest of your stay in town. The competition is tough, so the first encounter with a potential client is important, and drivers can be characterized by the methods they employ to capture a backpacker's heart.

THE CHARMER

The Charmer's million-dollar smile will make you wonder if you've arrived at a Miss Universe contest just in time for the charm competition. He'll answer your silly questions and smile all the time, accentuating his natural traits, hoping to charm or confuse you.

THE PHYSICAL

This type makes physical contact his go-to routine. The minute you get off the train or the bus, the Physical grabs your hand or puts his hands on your shoulder like he was an old friend, then ushers you to a quiet corner to close the deal.

THE SOPHISTICATE

The Sophisticate relies on longtime experience to identify backpackers' nationalities and establish instant intimacy. This is quite easy, since most travelers are Israelis, so he always starts speaking in Hebrew, the default language. It goes like this: You get off the train, calm and tranquil, then suddenly you hear a scream that shakes you: "Shalom, Israel!" (Hello, Israel!) You turn around, your ears still ringing, and discover a grinning simpleton who is certain that his linguistic skills have amazed you and captured your heart.

THE CONNECTOR

The Connector uses the same method as the Sophisticate, with one noticeable difference: he has an entire book of references in Hebrew, including photos of himself embraced by Shimon and Rachel from Tel Aviv, plus addresses and phone numbers of previous Israelis who have booked his services. He makes his living exclusively by serving the Israeli community and is considered especially reliable.

THE GENTLEMAN

The Gentleman does not push himself into the whole fuss. Instead, he waits in some far corner watching the turmoil around him. And how does he make his living? Well, his survival depends on the independent and resourceful travelers who cut through the turmoil at a decisive and rapid pace without looking at anyone. These travelers believe the rickshaw drivers crowded at the exits are experienced hands who will try to trick them. Most backpackers are terrified of the possibility of being tricked, so they cut through the mob of pushy drivers, looking for an inexperienced driver who scarcely speaks English, certain that this poor guy would be grateful to take them for a low fee. Little do they know that the Gentleman Driver is the most ruthless of the lot and will not hesitate to double or even triple the regular price—always with a polite smile.

THE SHADOW

The Shadow is the Indian version of the perfect salesman who never gives up. In Agra, where the Taj Mahal is located, our Shadow never left us for a second. We cut left, and he was with us; right, and he was there. We got out of the bus terminal, climbed over a bridge, crossed a busy intersection, did everything we could to shake him off, but he never wavered. He was there with us like some basic element of nature, whispering his charming offers in a soft and enticing tone. We decided to test his limits. The Taj Mahal is an hour by train from Agra, and it did not make sense to walk there with our backpacks in the sweltering heat, but to make the point, we started walking along a dirty canal. The Shadow stared at us, shocked, then recovered fast, got into his rickshaw, and began to chase us, urging us to hire him with the same soft, caressing voice. After five minutes we gave up and climbed in.

THE STUDENT

The Student appeals to the respect and sense of guilt any Western tourist feels in the face of the local population's misery. He introduces himself as a poor student who is studying to become a doctor that will help his epidemic-stricken people. To fund his studies, he works as a rickshaw driver. Every rupee he makes will support his studies, and that sums it up.

THE AGGRESSIVE

The Aggressive Driver has no time for games and nonsense. The minute he spots you, he signals for you to get in the rickshaw already. One cannot negotiate price with this driver, since he is a working man, a real professional who cannot waste time on idle talk.

THE NEEDY

India has a wide scope of these creative types, who have heartbreaking stories about their kids, their wives, and all sorts of medical emergencies. Given some of the hair-raising stories we've heard in these rickshaws, it is a medical wonder that some of these people were able to drive at all.

There are innumerable combinations of the types listed above; some better, some worse. The volatile mix of the Aggressive and the Physical is hardly recommended, and blending elements of the Shadow and the Charmer produces a character straight out of a horror movie. The most effective fusions seem to be the Student and the Gentleman or the Sophisticated and the Needy—an irresistible combination.

Of all the rickshaw drivers we met in the East, Muhammad was the only one we bonded with. When we arrived at Jaipur's dusty bus terminal, we were approached by a young man in the Student category who agreed to take us to a hostel for a ridiculously low price. The Student spoke good English, which we attributed to his intensive medical studies. We explained our policy regarding driving the rickshaw—no blind turns, no crazy races with truck drivers, and no talking to us while driving by turning his head to the back of the rickshaw, a life-shortening habit.

The Student nodded gallantly and repeated out loud all our safe driving tips, as if he was surprised that he had not considered them before.

We felt much better, until the Student took us to his psychedelically painted rickshaw and introduced the real driver, who didn't speak any English, overtook other vehicles in impossible situations, tried to win crazy races with truck drivers, and kept turning back every second to stare at Odelia.

We got off the rickshaw with shaking legs and in weak pantomime informed the young psychopath that at nine o'clock sharp the next morning we expected to see the original student, and no one else! The energetic lunatic nodded as if he understood every word. This was the last time we ever saw the Student or his elusive cousin.

The next morning, we received our story's main protagonist instead: the *capo di tutti i capi* (the boss of all bosses) of the rickshaw drivers in Jaipur: Muhammad.

When Muhammad met us at the hotel entrance that first day, he was the embodiment of the resilient spirit that enables India to endure and move forward despite adversity.

Muhammad was about fifty, of average height and protruding belly. He wore a worn-out undershirt that was white in a previous life; it seemed that the last time he shaved was around the time Mahatma Gandhi was assassinated. But his eyes were warm and intelligent. He somehow looked different from the other rickshaw drivers. He agreed to the rate we offered him for the coming week without any negotiation, and so we began our acquaintance. Through conversations during our rides in fluent English, we started to get to know the person behind the driver, and we learned that Muhammad had been a victim of a bittersweet fate.

The ancient Greeks could have written a tragic drama about his life story, but Muhammad endured his fate with surprising equanimity. His quandary? The fact that his wife had given birth to six girls.

Six girls, however beautiful and devoted to their parents (as we saw in the photos plastered to the roof of Muhammad's rickshaw), represent a heavy financial burden in India. When a daughter is about to get married and move into her husband's house, the bride's father is expected to help the young couple. The lower the amount the father can provide to the bride's family, the less chance of a decent match. In contrast, a son continues the family tradition, becomes the economic support for his elderly parents, and receives help from his bride's father when he gets married.

Each time another girl was born, Muhammad's future debt swelled. The eldest daughter married a young man who worked in a local factory. The burden was heavy, but Muhammad managed. The second daughter, the prettiest of all, agreed to a match Muhammad arranged for her— an elderly man, quite well-to-do, who did not ask for any help when he saw the bride's beauty.

The real challenge began with the third daughter, who fell in love with an educated guy from a different caste. He wanted to marry her, but his parents refused to consider this inappropriate match without a sizable gift from Muhammad and his wife. When all hope was gone, Muhammad took a loan with painfully high interest to secure the marriage.

At this point, Muhammad told us, he knew that if he did not take extreme measures, he would not be able to help his three younger daughters, which could force them into solitary lives. In a surprising and bold move, he boarded a cargo ship to Europe, knowing he would never be able to make enough money in India. He worked as a sous chef on the ship to pay for the journey, then stayed in Europe for eight full years, working as a cook in Indian restaurants in London, Brussels, and Paris. He lived sparingly, and every month he sent money to his family in Jaipur and prayed he would be able to go back soon. With the money he sent, his wife managed to marry off another daughter, pay back the loan they had taken out, and buy a small, modest house where she lived with their two younger daughters.

He returned to India proud of his enormous achievement. Two daughters were left unmarried, and if neither repeated the middle daughter's revolt, he had no doubt they could find decent husbands. He bought a rickshaw and drove backpackers around the city.

Everything looked nice and cozy, but Muhammad started to see that he had to pay another price for his success and boldness: the price of comparison. Before he went to Europe, he had never left his hometown. He loved Jaipur and had been happy and content with his living situation, his friends, and the general atmosphere. But the trip to Europe exposed him to things he had never dreamt of. He saw the Eiffel Tower, watched the changing of the guards at Buckingham Palace, and walked around beautiful parks in Europe's capitals. But most importantly, he saw how other people lived, and the contrast between clean, rich Western Europe and poor, crowded India was at times painful and unbearable.

He realized how dirty his beloved Jaipur was. He noticed with fresh eyes the swarms of beggars who filled the streets. He saw the black diesel fumes from trucks and buses that filled the air with suffocating pollution. It dawned on him that he was destined to live as a simple rickshaw driver who battled, day in and day out, the killer traffic, the horrific congestion, the blackening pollution, while knowing that elsewhere life could be much better. He decided to fight human nature, accepting everything around him with an open mind. This brave mental process had taken a long time, but Muhammad was an optimist who understood that he was destined to bear the curse of comparing his former life to his current situation, driving his rickshaw under the ruthless sun.

He kept his calm, but from time to time when a mocking devil suppressed his efforts, his curiosity would rise to the surface, prompting him to start conversations about his former life. It would start with an idle conversation, masking his deep longing for unattainable Europe.

"So, have you ever been in Paris?" he would ask us while driving, his eyes on the traffic before him.

"We have, several times," we answered.

Muhammad would nod as if he'd expected such a response. "Gardens of Luxembourg?"

"Yes, nice gardens indeed."

"Nice? Is that what you call them?" Muhammad would get excited. "These are the most beautiful gardens in the world. Such flowers, the color of the grass, the royal fountains, free concerts . . ." His words trailed off as he drove his rickshaw.

After some time, compelled to save him from his sour mood, we tried to shift the conversation back to his reality.

"You know, India also has some beautiful public gardens."

"How can you even compare?" he would utter contemptuously. "Here everything is dirty, filthy, full of people, beasts, and monkeys. There, it's a real civilization, but here it is . . ." He would be quiet for a moment, slithering through the heavy traffic. "Here it is . . ."

"More authentic?" we would offer.

"Authentic?" Muhammad would mutter in inexplicable fury. "You call this folkloric?" He would lift his hands off the wheel and make a large gesture. "No, no, sir, this is not authentic. It's a jungle! Just a crazy jungle!"

One day we decided to invite him to a local branch of Pizza Hut. Muhammad was excited, as the restaurant was too expensive for him. All the way he described the many pizzas he had had in Europe with all the different toppings. When we arrived at the restaurant, though, he changed his tune, informing us that he could not accept our generous invitation.

"If I give in to my impulse now," he said, mortified, "my longing to luxury would overcome me. My life would be unbearable."

We accepted his logic and entered the air-conditioned, spotlessly clean restaurant. The place was an exact replica of any branch in the US, with English menus on the tables and waiters dressed in uniforms.

Our waiter told us that he was a university graduate. "Because of the enormous demand for a job in the chain, only applicants with a bachelor's degree have been accepted," he informed us. While we were considering our order—Greek pizza with feta cheese, capers, and mozzarella, or a tropical pizza with fresh pineapple slices—a turmoil started at the entrance. Screams, shoves, the security guy holding someone who was trying to get into the restaurant. Someone called the manager, who rushed out of his office, his striped suit flying, his flip-flops stiff on the cold marble floor. Amidst the crowd's circle, a white worn-out undershirt emerged.

Muhammad.

He held the reception desk like an altar, with his hands stretched out and his head lowered, while the guard towered over him, trying to detach him from the desk. The manager was banging Muhammad's head with a plastic flip-flop. It was hard to convince everyone that Muhammad had arrived to eat with us. The employees were speechless as Muhammad rose, a winner. He straightened his thin hair while staring at the manager, as if to say, "Look here, I may look like a poor rickshaw driver, but I know how to enjoy what life has to offer."

At the table, Muhammad ordered a large pizza with sausage, which he ate with obvious pleasure. We never dared to ask what made him change his mind.

Over the following days, Muhammad spoke no more about Europe. He appeared to be in a more forgiving mood, showing us his favorite spots in his beloved town while graciously ignoring the bad traffic, the pollution, the endless swarms of people everywhere. We spent another week in Jaipur until its heat and humidity weighed us down. We decided to fly to the Indian Himalayas, a cool, refreshing location far from the chaos that characterized Jaipur. We wished to travel in Ladakh, at the Tibet-India border, during the short summertime there.

We packed our backpacks. Muhammad took us to the bus station. When we said our goodbyes, he gave us a small package wrapped in a filthy brown rag.

"Take it. It's for you, for everything you have done for me," he said, his eyes beaming. "Don't open it until you leave Jaipur."

The bus departed and we saw him standing on the sidewalk, waving at us. When his figure disappeared and Jaipur was far behind us, we opened the package. Inside, wrapped in a soft white cloth, rested a small green marble statue of the Eiffel Tower in Paris.

CHAPTER FOUR

THE KINGDOM OF THE MOON

AT THE DELHI AIRPORT, WAITING for the flight that would carry us to Leh, Ladakh's capital, we made friends with a young Indian who was fluent in English. He led groups of European mountain climbers and advised us to stay at the Tessring family's guest house in Leh.

"It's a typical Ladakhi family with deep roots there," Manush told us. He knew them well, as his father had served in the military with Dorje, the patriarch of the family.

"How can a Tibetan Buddhist who stands for nonviolence serve in the army?" we wondered, but we never received an answer. Even after staying a whole month with the Tessrings, we could not understand this discrepancy.

The airplane flew over the snowy peaks of the Himalayas, crossed over the endless desert, and landed at Leh.

Ladakh is an enchanted region. When you look up you see barren monasteries perched in lofty and forsaken mountain peaks. Looking around you, you see the orange and yellow robes of Buddhist monks among patches of emerald-green fields amidst the desert landscape. Tibetan prayers, along with horn blows and hypnotizing drumbeats, are the soundtrack that comes all day from the monasteries.

A deserted stone palace looks over the town.

The British archeologist General Alexander Cunningham visited Ladakh at the end of the nineteenth century and described it as a "wasteland to an unbelievable extent. From above, Ladakh seems like a collection of yellow plains and barren mountains covered with snow." All these years later, nothing much had changed. Ladakh presented to us the same glorious views of bare valleys with no vegetation, a wild place that cannot be managed, just adapted to, a location that invokes awe of the raw power of this high desert in the midst of the Himalayas.

Ladakh is the highest plateau in India, with an elevation of 10,000 feet above sea level and a minimal amount of precipitation. These conditions make it an elevated snowy desert. The white mountain peaks form a stark and poignant contrast to the barren view. The short summer season is the best time to tour the area; during the bitter winter, its lofty, snowy mountains are impassable, and the temperatures drop well below zero.

The kingdom of Ladakh used to be part of the ancient Silk Road between India, Tibet, and Central Asia; it is now in a complicated and sensitive situation. Geographically, it belongs to the huge Tibetan Plateau, part of the Kashmir region that is at the center of a border dispute between India and Pakistan. While the region is part of India, the dominant religion is Tibetan Buddhism.

Like the legendary Mustang region in Nepal, Ladakhi citizens keep a traditional Buddhist way of life, with all its rituals. That is why Ladakh is called Little Tibet, a nickname that was cemented in 1987 when the Dalai Lama started spending his summers there in the Thikse Monastery.

We strolled in the town for a long while, searching for the Tessring family's house. After numerous inquiries we found it. It was surrounded by a large garden that grew tomatoes and potatoes. An older woman who was working in the garden rushed to wipe her hands when she noticed us, greeting us with the traditional *"jullay"* that means hello, goodbye, or thank you, depending on the situation. She looked to be about fifty, average height, her long hair braided. When she smiled, she exposed beautiful white teeth. This was Dolma, Dorje's wife. Later we met her charismatic husband, their daughters, and their son, Jimmy, a local teen idol.

Dolma ushered us to a simple, clean room and invited us to join her family for a cup of Tibetan butter tea. As we sat in the spacious garden under a broad tree that cooled down the desert heat, the tip of a braid interlaced with colorful beads appeared at the far corner of the balcony. I continued to drink the horrific, salty butter tea, pretending I had not seen anything. When she was sure no one had seen her, the little girl became confident and slowly revealed her features: a small pug nose, high cheekbones, slanted eyes. Her pretty braid caught most of our attention. It moved as if it had a life of its own, like a snake searching for sunlight to warm itself in. The braid's owner turned out to be Dolkar, Dorje's little daughter. Her sister's name was Diskreet, and they were so much alike that I could not distinguish between them during the entire month I spent at the house. They accepted this confusion with an understanding smile.

We met Dorje in the evening. He was a short man with typical Tibetan features, muscular and flexible like a snow tiger. A few minutes before he arrived we heard him singing from afar. Every evening the entire family would gather by the gate to welcome him back from his travels around the region. He would arrive full of energy, talking to every one of his children with the most attentive ear. Dorje owned ten yaks and used them to transport heavy loads from village to village for his day job. In the evenings, he was the principal dancer in a traditional dance group that revived ancient Ladakhi dances. They performed all over India and had even received an official invitation to perform in Mongolia.

Dorje was full of natural, easy charm. He treated his family with exceptional kindness, always smiling, oftentimes singing. He had served in the army for fifteen years, and with the money saved he built his spacious home. He was a fanatic keeper of local tradition and had deep pride in the ancient traditions, unique clothes, dancing, and jewelry of Ladakh. On the roof of his house he'd built a small temple in which he kept various prayer articles that had been passed down from one generation to the next.

When we wondered about the conflict of interests between serving in the army and observing the Buddhist doctrine of nonviolence, he shrugged. He said he'd fulfilled his duty to defend the Ladakhi borders against China's aspirations for the region.

In 1979 when the first civil plane landed in Ladakh, it shook up the entire area. Every conversation we had with him turned toward the time when the life of his small, isolated community had changed forever.

"Nineteen seventy-nine," Dorje would say, stressing each syllable. "Nineteen seventy-nine is the year when we understood how the world regarded us, the Ladakhi citizens: as a medieval community that lived with no electricity or running water, along with a rich spiritual life that is abundant in rituals, symbolism, and Tantric Buddhism."

Dorje would talk at length about the time before tourists discovered Ladakh. "Until that first plane landed, everyone used to leave their houses unlocked. If anyone needed anything from their neighbor, they could come by any time, taking whatever they needed."

From his stories we learned about how life had been in the tight community when everyone followed the ancient traditions. I had no doubt that if he could travel back in time, Dorje would do so without hesitation. At our first dinner with the family we met Jigmat, the elder son. We were promised by his proud mother that he would put on a singing and dancing show for us. Dolma had told us that her son was fifteen years old; she added, smiling widely, the words "many girls." We had no idea what she meant until he showed up at dinner. He was a handsome lad who looked more like a teen idol than the son of a hardworking Tibetan family. Jigmat, or Jimmy, as he liked to be called, was tall and blessed with shiny straight hair, honey-hued eyes with long lashes, and amazing dimples. He knew he was handsome and did not try to hide behind false modesty.

When we asked him if he would dance for us, Jimmy jumped from his seat, went straight to his room, and returned with a tape cassette that he inserted into a battered recorder on the floor. He pushed different buttons, but to no avail—until he beat the tape hard and it started to work. To our surprise, the music was not Ladakhi, but Indian pop music by Alisha, with her hit "Made in India," a catchy song mixing Hindi and English. Jimmy started shaking his shoulders like a Bollywood actor, narrowing his eyes from time to time to create the proper effect. He moved his elastic body to the beat of the music, making all the gestures one would expect from a young rock star. The performance was perfect, and at the end of the show we all applauded with enthusiasm. Jimmy bowed to us, his dimples deepening.

Dorje did not join the celebration; he retired early to his room.

When we talked to Jimmy, we learned that he was influenced by Indian teachers from New Delhi. They had a strong Western orientation and regarded the Buddhist Ladakhi children as coming from another, less sophisticated era. Jimmy was also influenced by the international tourists who arrived every summer to bask in the calming beauty of this unique, spiritual region. All these tourists, us included, were millionaires compared to the local population. We walked along the narrow streets equipped with expensive mountain shoes, excellent coats, and valuable cameras. The Ladakhi youth stared at this abundance with wide-eyed astonishment. For the local youngsters, we represented a dream, some fuzzy ideal life that would enable them to escape to the modern world. Of course, they did not recognize the irony that we'd paid quite a bit to travel from afar to the same place they wanted to escape from.

A few days after we arrived at the Tessrings', we witnessed a bitter argument between Jigmat and Dorje when Jimmy demanded money from his father to enroll in a new fitness center.

Dorje was dumbfounded. He turned to his son, shaking his head. "I don't understand it. What is this fitness center?"

Jigmat looked at him as if considering the merit of this conversation. Then he said, "It's a place to become stronger, to put up some muscles on my body."

Dorje again shook his head in disbelief.

"You need to pay someone to become stronger?" he asked in an incredulous tone. "Look at me." He showed Jigmat the solid muscles on his forearms, borne of hard labor over many years. "Come work with me. You will get all the muscles you need."

Jigmat did not respond, but Dorje did not give in. At last Jimmy relented, but we wondered how long that victory would last.

Most travelers pass through Leh without lingering there, regarding the Ladakhi capital as a starting point for trips into the snowy desert, but Odelia and I were enchanted by the town and wished to learn more about the culture. We ended up staying with the Tessrings for a month. Odelia became a close friend of the two young daughters, who were eager to hear stories about the West. Diskreet wanted to become a flight attendant; Dolkar dreamt about fashion design. Odelia, who had once been a flight attendant as well as a fashion designer, was a curious realization of both of their dreams. Even though she repeated the same stories about her past every time they sat together, the girls listened to every word, their eyes shining, imagining splendid faraway worlds.

Though they were almost the same age, Dorje's daughters were quite different from one another. Diskreet was the life of the house, always surrounded by other children, the center of constant commotion. Dolkar, on the other hand, was reserved. The path to Dolkar's heart was through an old guitar Odelia found in one of the rooms, left there by a backpacker who gave up on her dream of becoming a musician. Odelia would sit under a large tree, strum the guitar, and sing classics such as "Hotel California." Dolkar loved sitting by Odelia and listening to the music. This spontaneous get-together became a daily ritual, and Dorje and Dolma observed the bonding between Odelia and Dolkar with a satisfied nod.

One night when we were sound asleep, strange sounds of groaning, snorting, and grunting woke us up. The pavilion we slept in was a bit distanced from the main house, and when we went out, we found several donkeys devouring the vegetables in the Tessrings' gardens. While I tried to chase them away, Odelia hurried to wake everyone up. Within minutes the family showed up with torches and sticks to scare off the donkeys. We'd saved the vegetable garden, and in return we received their heartfelt gratitude.

We often joined the Tessring family for visits to nearby villages that were much less touristy. There we met their siblings; warm, welcoming people who did not speak any English. Everywhere we went we were offered the same salty, awful Tibetan tea. Occasionally I assisted Dorje in his chores around the house, and sometimes I accompanied him to the high grazing fields in the lofty mountains to shepherd his small herd of yaks.

We would sit on the mountainside looking at a huge granite wall that seemed to go on forever. In the distance, a snowy mountain peak was glowing. I sat quietly by Dorje's side, trying to absorb his tranquility. He was one of these rare people that aroused instant respect, someone you wanted to impress, whose appreciation you wanted to win. One morning as we were sitting at ease, eating dried cheese and a round wheat cake Dolma had baked for us, Dorje asked me why Odelia and I were traveling for such a long time. My default answer to this question, that this was all "before the kids and the mortgage," somehow didn't feel right this time. I told him we wanted to taste what real freedom was like.

He smiled his noble smile and said nothing.

After a few minutes of sitting quietly I asked him what he thought about our trip around the world. He looked at the mountains for another long moment before he spoke. "Freedom is inside, here," he said, touching his heart with his left palm. "I was free even when I served in the Indian army for fifteen years." He saluted an imaginary captain, then continued. "If you chase freedom, it will run away."

I was embarrassed.

Dorje noticed my uneasiness and said with a smile, "Anyone who comes here rushes to see the past, our old monasteries. They do not try to understand us, the people who live here. You are different. You stayed with us, didn't go anywhere else." He patted my shoulder. "It's good." He laughed. I smiled back, and he patted my shoulder again with another broad smile.

A light wind started to blow. When Dorje finished eating, he began to sculpt a piece of wood with his knife. He whistled, focusing on his creation. When he finished, he handed me an accurate representation of the scenery we were looking at. It was an amazing depiction of the barren landscape in front of us. I smiled, thanking him for the gift, and he nodded in satisfaction.

While staying in Leh, we learned more about this fascinating place. The kingdom had been isolated for many years, during which the Ladakhi people established an independent society with stiff social and ecological rules that enabled survival in an unforgiving area. The Buddhist faith was the common denominator for its hardworking inhabitants until the establishment of Indian military bases and the appearance of Western tourists changed their lifestyles. The Ladakhis did not have it easy. Their daily work was physically demanding, their winters brutal, their public infrastructure nonexistent. Nevertheless, it seemed that the Ladakhi joy of life stood well against the daily hardships. We never saw them bitter or frustrated. The Ladakhis were optimistic people who smiled easily, naturally. When they smiled, their hearts smiled as well, their faces glowing with the joy of life they were blessed with.

Was it their compassionate Buddhist faith that enabled the faithful to deal with this tough life? Or did the Ladakhis have an especially moderate temperament? We had no idea, but life with the family had a blissful effect on us. We felt happy when we were with them, realizing that you don't need much in life to be content.

We spent our last afternoon in Leh on the balcony enjoying the strong tea that Dolkar brewed for us after her daily music lesson with Odelia. We had no idea that those were our last hours there.

The wind was blowing softly, the Tibetan gongs sounding in the distance. The sweet smell of the flowers growing undisturbed in the large garden filled the air. The sun shone gently on our faces; everything around us was enchanted. We felt so good in that place, so whole and perfect, that for a while we dozed off to a sweet nap.

A car's rattle woke us up and we looked down to see a battered jeep stop in front of the house. The door of the jeep opened, and Noshad, along with his glorious mustache, got out. Noshad was the driver we'd hired to take us to Manali, a resort town deep in the Himalayas. We'd booked his service through an agent, not knowing exactly when he would show up.

The Indian driver's arrival announced the end of our time in Leh with the Tessrings. Strong bonds now connected us with those wonderful caring people. This modest family had taken care of all our needs nobly and generously, unlike anything we had experienced before.

When we said goodbye, darkness was descending, the full moon shining above the snowy mountain peaks. We had to leave at that hour to avoid military blockages because Noshad did not have the permits necessary to drive passengers from Leh to Manali. We did not have time to prepare the family for our sudden departure, so it was an unpleasant surprise for them. When we loaded our stuff into the car, they all stood around us: Dorje, Dolma, Diskreet, and Jimmy. All but Dolkar, who preferred to lock herself up in her room, ignoring Odelia's pleas for her to come out.

The family embraced us warmly. Dolma took off an ancient necklace that adorned her neck and handed it to Odelia, who graciously accepted it. We got into the jeep and looked behind. We felt we were leaving our own family behind, that we had not exhausted our stay with them. We could have stayed longer, but we did not. Through the back window we saw them waving at us, and we felt a pang in our hearts.

CHAPTER FIVE

HANGING BY A THREAD

THE BACKPACKERS WE'D TALKED TO had warned us that the road from Leh in the Indian Himalayas to Manali in Northern India would be a once-in-a-lifetime experience. It was only three hundred miles, but it would take two full days to complete the treacherous trip.

Most of the journey is on a winding, mostly unpaved mountain road, about twelve feet wide, that is only open during the short summer season before the snow arrives. The road begins in a huge, snowy desert wasteland etched by deep valleys. It cuts through endless yellow flatlands walled in by lofty granite mountains and curves through high, snowy passes—including the second-highest mountain pass in the world that may be crossed by vehicle—then tears down the high desert on the Tibetan Plateau, clinging to mountain slopes like a roller coaster designed by an evil engineer, to emerge into green forests and fertile valleys. The words required to describe the trip can be found in the lexicon of a thriller writer: *shuddering, scary, breathtaking, shocking.*

In summer, thousands of military trucks bring food and equipment to the troops in Leh that protect the border from a possible Chinese or Pakistani invasion. Every encounter with these trucks becomes a game of chicken set against the backdrop of the magnificent Indian Himalayas.

Two options were available to us for this trip: a rickety, overcrowded bus that would most likely break down along the punishing road, or a more expensive hired driver in the local version of an American jeep.

The passengers on an Indian bus are at the driver's mercy. If he wishes, the driver may drive an entire day without stopping once—or get thoroughly drunk, or decide to use his left foot only. In an Indian bus, the driver is God, and the way he drives determines whether his passengers live or die. It's that simple, and until you get on the bus, you won't know if you happened to fall in with one of the more reasonable drivers, or if your driver gets a sadistic pleasure from the terrified screams of Western tourists when the bus hangs on the verge of an abyss. Like every other backpacker in India, we had our share of horror stories featuring long, nauseating bus rides breathing toxic fumes, and we had formed a theory about the drivers. An Indian bus driver drives as if he must prove his unshaken belief in reincarnation. The most reckless drivers seem to believe that their next life will be much better, so why worry about self-preservation?

After a few long bus rides, we started to wonder if the abysmal condition of the roads and the lack of enforcement of driving laws were a desperate attempt by the government to control population growth. India is expected to surpass China as the most populated country in the world, and unlike China, India's attempts to control the birth rate have all failed.

An insightful visitor can expect to spend many interesting hours watching the various ways one can get killed or seriously injured on Indian roads—and the spectator is not immune to the dangers. This is part of India's charm: no discrimination. Everyone has an equal opportunity to be killed in a traffic accident aided by several dreadful factors: driving conventions, drivers, means of transportation, number of people jam-packed into each vehicle, general road conditions, night rides, and Tata trucks.

Driving rules in India are realized as survival of the fittest. The first to get crushed are pedestrians and cyclists. Following them on the danger scale are scooters, rickshaws, motorcycles, cars, jeeps, minibuses, buses, and Tata trucks.

The only creature that can wander the streets immune to injury is the cow, which may stop the flow of traffic at any time—but until a cow shows up, the streets are a jungle. You crush everyone under you until a bigger predator arrives to crush you.

The rickshaw driver totally ignores pedestrians, bikers, and scooters, but becomes hyperalert when he detects a minibus in the rearview mirror. The minibus driver is calm. He cuts a clear path through the mayhem without slowing down or even blinking. Motorcyclists and bike riders move to the side of the road for him at the last second, and sometimes fall into the ditch. But the minibus driver's apathy evaporates as soon as a big predator—a bus or a Tata truck—appears.

All the trucks in India are made by the giant Tata corporation. These vehicles cut through hordes of scooters, rickshaws, and motorcycles like a Russian nuclear icebreaker cutting through thick ice.

For unexplained reasons, Tata trucks have a small front window that limits the driver's field of vision and narrow wheels that limit traction on the road. These ghastly trucks, decorated with various ornaments, are equal in status to great ocean predators like the great white shark or killer whale. Their sole rival is the bus, and a clash between the two giants is a hair-raising sight.

The unofficial driving rules are straightforward:

1. Never slow down when a vehicle approaches you, even if barely one vehicle can get through the narrow road.

2. The car horn is not a safety tool but a musical instrument to be used frequently, without relation to the traffic conditions. Exceptions of this

rule are blind turns; in these cases, do not use
the horn at all.
3. Don't turn on the headlights in a night drive.

Drivers try to pack moving vehicles with as many people
as possible. Even in a fully crammed bus with all seats
occupied and standing posts jammed, a creative driver
will seat on the gear box a skinny boy who will move his
leg or elbow at each gear change.

When the bus is totally full and you are sure that the
trip is finally going to start, passengers start climbing up
to the roof. Before they cram together up there, they pile it
high with bags, suitcases, sharp iron pipes, timbers with
large rusty nails, and long heavy jute bags with obscure
content. Everything is tied up haphazardly, assuring free
movement during the ride. The passengers sit on all the
luggage, holding onto loose ropes on the roof's sides.

There is no doubt that the roof is the most dangerous
place on the bus. Every time the driver applies the brakes,
a hapless passenger falls off the roof. Tree branches and
electric wires reduce the number of passengers even more.
The sharp iron pipes wait patiently for the next victim to
impale on a sharp turn.

Only when the bus is packed solid does the ride begin
and a bus with a capacity of fifty begins to barrel down
the street with a hundred passengers.

In India, a street is a flexible concept. Sometimes it is
a paved roadway, but oftentimes it is jutted earth filled

with holes wide enough to swallow an entire vehicle. There are no guardrails or light posts. The bridges are old, rickety, and poorly maintained.

A large portion of road trips in India take place at night, so imagine the same old packed buses, crazy speed, violent hierarchy, driving conventions, and narrow roads with the unwelcome addition of dark nights and bleary-eyed drivers. During such trips, a passenger has endless opportunities to consider her life priorities, thinking warmly about all the things she wanted to do in life and likely will not be able to. One advertisement we saw on a tour bus in Delhi summed it all up: "Enjoy the adventure of being alive!"

We opted for the private jeep.

If we took a jeep with a private driver, we thought, we'd be able to control the situation. We'd be able to stop anytime we wished, paying the driver only at the end of the trip to give him an incentive to drive responsibly.

In no time, however, we found that this was not such an easy task. Local companies demanded a mint for the ride, and no one would split the cost with us.

After searching at length for a solution for us, Dorje learned that jeeps taking tourists the opposite way, from Manali to Leh, would sometimes pick up return passengers for half price, but a local regulation protecting union drivers forbade them to do so. Dorje said he would look for a driver willing to take the risk; we'd have to be patient, and when the driver was ready, we'd need to leave right then and there, on the spot.

A week passed. We started thinking that we would never leave Leh, and honestly, we liked the thought.

But then Noshad appeared. He was in his early twenties, dark-skinned, and had a curly, greased mustache that he kept strictly groomed. He spoke softly, nodding constantly, affirming everything we said. We laid before him our ten commandments for the trip:

1. Always drive slowly, especially when cornering.
2. Don't overtake other vehicles at blind turns.
3. Don't get too close to the vehicle in front of you.
4. When you see a vehicle coming toward you, slow down.
5. Turn on the lights at night.
6. Stay in the marked lane.
7. Stop the vehicle when asked to.
8. Don't pick up extra passengers on the way.
9. Stop for photo opportunities at special spots.
10. Respond to our requests.

Noshad nodded, repeating every rule as we uttered it, and we felt like this would be an easy, nice ride.

He told us that two Chinese photographers would join us. We agreed willingly and asked to see the famous jeep. Like a proud father, Noshad ushered us toward his Indian masterpiece, an accessorized Tata Sumo that, according to Noshad, had been released from the factory a week before.

When we looked at the odometer, we saw that the "new" jeep had already logged 100,000 miles.

A huge sculpture of Ganesh, the elephant-headed Hindu god of good luck who is also known as the remover of obstacles, was placed over the dashboard. Ganesh did a splendid job of hiding the windshield, but we guessed that the protection he offered his ardent believers would make up for this limited vision.

At three a.m. we found ourselves in the jeep with Noshad and Ganesh on our way to pick up the two Chinese ladies while avoiding the military blockage. Noshad navigated skillfully in the town's narrow streets till we reached the meeting point. To our surprise, instead of Chinese photographers, we found an interesting-looking Western couple waiting for us at the corner. The young woman was wrapped up in an ornamental rag through which we could only see her clear blue eyes. The guy was short and plump, with a thick beard covering most of his face. At first sight he looked like an experienced traveler. He wore red cotton pants and a thin yellow blanket over a long white cotton shirt. He had an impressive collection of rings, bracelets, necklaces, and earrings; presumably souvenirs from his adventures around the world, carried like calcium deposits on the body of a humpback whale. On his right hand he wore a huge ruby that looked like a signet ring belonging to a ruler of an enchanted tropical island. On his forefinger was a snake fighting a dragon. It wasn't clear who was winning.

On his right ear were three triangular metal earrings, each engraved with a Sanskrit word. The left ear was adorned with a metal hoop that seemed as if it had been stolen from a lion tamer. The crown jewel of his collection was a copper pendant in the shape of a marijuana leaf with tiny, delicate bells on the sides. The pendant hung on a rusty chain around his neck, rattling with every step he took.

The bearded guy opened the jeep's back door, and when he saw us staring at him curiously, he greeted us with a joyful "Good morning!"

We nodded politely, then heard him talking to his girlfriend in perfect Hebrew: "*Yallah, yallah* (come on, come on), start loading."

Turned out that our travel partners were Shimon and Keren, who expected to be traveling with a couple of professional photographers. This was what our mysterious driver had promised them. A few minutes after we hit the road, it became obvious that behind Shimon's intimidating appearance was a simple guy traveling outside Israel for the first time in his life. He had been in India for two weeks, and the transformation he'd undergone in this time was remarkable. He showed me his photo from the time he arrived in New Delhi wearing a flannel shirt over a white T-shirt. In Delhi he'd acquired the colorful outfit he was wearing and purchased the rings, bracelets, necklaces, and earrings from a local merchant.

The marijuana leaf was a gift from a backpacker he met for a brief moment.

Only several days after landing in Delhi, Shimon looked like an experienced world traveler.

This is one of India's many advantages: one may assimilate within a few hours. Throw off your previous clothing, add a few pounds of necklaces, cover yourself with colorful local outfits, and gain a new, exotic look. Anywhere else in the Western world you'd be classified as a hippie rebel, but the beauty of India is that there are no classifications. There is an unbelievable diversity of characters, clothes, jewelry, turbans, and colors. Whatever you do, you will never stand out.

Noshad started the car, shifted to first gear, and began driving. Keren opened her bag, pulled out a cassette, and tossed it skillfully toward Noshad with the cry, "*Babu*, play this music!"

The cassette hit Noshad's forehead, who was astonished at the juxtaposition of an old Indian word of respect and being struck by a cassette. He momentarily lost control of the jeep and it spun out of control. A long wall of Buddhist prayer wheels loomed ahead of us as Noshad tried frantically to get control of the steering wheel. I held Odelia tight, expecting an impact. The jeep swerved madly until it stopped, brakes screeching, in front of the prayer wheels. Odelia was pale, holding my hand tightly. Later she said she had been wondering what crashing into the prayer wheels would have meant. Was it positive or negative karma?

Noshad was shocked. From the back we heard giggling, then the two lovebirds exploded with laughter. Keren, holding her tummy joyfully, released the next pearl toward dumbfounded Noshad: "*Babu*, driver number one in India!"

The original meaning of the popular word *babu* in Hindu is a respectful way to address the patriarch of a family. This word is uttered with profound reverence among Indians, especially when addressing an elder. Indians will lower their voice and sometimes bow their head when using this word. However, some backpackers have adopted this word, treating it as a local version of "buddy" or "bro."

So, with an old tape cassette flying over our driver's head, our weird journey to Manali started. I believe that this opening episode resulted in a few loose screws in Noshad's head, but I can't be sure.

Noshad pulled himself together, started the jeep, and returned to the rocky path that curled through the dry desert landscape. He had to rush through the first checkpoint before the military forces got there. He drove fast along the curved way, clouds of dust behind us. Shimon and Keren slept peacefully in the back, their colorful blankets covering them completely. At dawn we arrived in yellow meadows surrounded by snowy mountain peaks that reminded us we were in one of the highest spots in the world. Wild, primal nature surrounded us, with no human intervention, not even a temporary tent camp.

The military checkpoint was empty, and as soon as we passed it, Noshad calmed down and asked Keren to hand him the tape. He must have decided to let bygones be bygones. But as soon as he inserted the tape into the cassette deck, we heard a loud boom and the car filled with smoke. Noshad stopped the jeep and we all ran out, coughing from the thick smoke that was pouring from the cassette deck.

This mysterious accident set off Noshad's behavior for the rest of the trip. Maybe it was the final nail in the coffin for him, the trigger for his bizarre moods; our meek driver started to act strange. He disregarded the rules we had set up for him: refused to slow down when vehicles approached, never honked at blind turns, drove ever faster on the loose gravel that passed for a road. Noshad was a free spirit, bent on deviating from the main road, trying unmarked paths at every opportunity.

Whenever he spotted a dangerous path, he turned onto it without a second thought, like an intrepid explorer in search of adventure. We would be driving toward a mountain pass when, without any warning, he would cut left or right into a steep slope, the jeep jumping over rocks like a mountain goat. When we asked why he was making such awkward descents off the main path, all he would say was "Faster, faster."

After a while we became used to these descents, and even anticipated some of them. But we could not get used to Noshad's habit of abandoning the steering wheel whenever he lost control of the jeep. He would drop his hands to his sides and look at us with surprise, like a father who cannot control his wayward daughter. The jeep would shake violently from side to side until Noshad somehow recovered and managed to hold the wheel with both hands. These dangerous seconds felt like eternity every time.

Noshad was adamant that we must arrive at a desolate town named Keylong on the first day of the trip. He told us that a good friend of his was waiting for us there with "good food." To do that, we had to drive for ten hours on dangerous dirt roads, but Noshad refused to consider any other option. We stopped for lunch at a random collection of tents that had been set up in the middle of the desert as an improvised stop. The camp was manned by a Nepalese family that wasn't deterred by the fierce cold of this empty wasteland.

We got into one of the tents, and through the corner of our eye saw Noshad being swallowed into a large tent on the hilltop. He came out of that tent after two hours, obviously content. This delay cost us dearly, and when we set out again, he accelerated even more.

Two hours after we left the tent camp, we arrived at another mountain pass. The narrow, winding road was a series of precarious switchbacks that offered the only passage to the mountain's peak. There was no room for mistake; we watched the deep ravines on our left side and waited for Noshad to career off the road.

The route wound around the cliffs like a snake; the air was cold as a banker refusing a loan to a dubious client; the shadowy valley below waited with endless patience for a moment of distraction. Noshad was now driving wildly, taking the narrow turns at top speed, braking sharply, raising hellish clouds of dust, letting go of the wheel for nerve-racking seconds, catching it back, then accelerating out of the turn.

Shimon and Keren encouraged these feats with roars and enthusiastic leg stamping. Noshad got bolder, faster.

"Promise me," Odelia demanded in a quiet, stressed voice, "that if we arrive in Manali safely, we will take a meditation course."

I nodded, promising myself that if we survived this trip, I would become a better person, more grateful for the life I was given. Noshad's driving was suitable for a European off-road rally. Shimon and Keren were ecstatic, cheering him on with rhythmical calls: "Faster, *babu*, faster!" I screamed at him to slow down, but he ignored me. His eyes were glazed and he was mumbling a strange, monotonous prayer, probably aimed at the elephant god that obstructed the front window. Odelia held the tiny book of psalms she had pulled out of her bag. She was white as a sheet. I hugged her, not knowing what to do.

The nightmare continued. Another impossible turn, letting go of the wheel again, another near-death experience.

Night fell upon us like a quiet predator. We could not see the abyss beneath us anymore, but my imagination filled in the blanks. Whenever the jeep tilted to one side or the other, I felt spasms in my stomach. I remembered the roller coaster at Disneyland in Orlando. There too the ride is in total darkness, so one never knows when the next turn or descent is. Despite the real fear you feel at such an experience, you know the roller coaster is tested regularly and that the Walt Disney Company would never risk the safety of the riders and end up in a multimillion–dollar lawsuit. Who could you sue here? I thought bitterly to myself. If something happened, Noshad would fall to the abyss with the rest of us.

Time passed by like an old man climbing a steep hill. Finally, in the distance we saw twinkling lights.

"Keylong," murmured Noshad. "Keylong."

In the remote town, Noshad drove confidently on the narrow streets until we climbed toward a dimly lit building atop a steep hill. He reached the top of the hill at full speed and hit a rickety wooden shed that held a large pile of apples. The shed screeched under the attack but stayed put. Noshad stepped on the gas pedal and the poor shed broke apart. For a splendid second, the apple pile stayed put, then it collapsed and a rain of apples covered the car.

At last we arrived at the hotel. Shimon got out of the jeep in a springy leap and walked in, wrapped up in his blanket like a bear. The little bells around the marijuana leaf made soft sounds, his curls swayed as he moved, his smiling eyes flickered through his beard. He looked like an energetic raccoon.

I followed him to the hotel, where he addressed the manager without any hint of hesitation.

"*Babu*, how much room here?"

The manager stared at him.

Shimon repeated his question, stressing every word as if talking to a child.

The manager did not respond at first. After a while he murmured, "Two hundred rupees a night."

Shimon patted the manager's shoulder and looked him in the eye, speaking slowly. "*Babu*, how much the price for me, not for other people?"

"Two hundred rupees a night . . ." murmured the manager.

Shimon's hand moved from the manager's shoulder and patted the back of his head.

"We pay you one hundred rupees a night," he stated. "Please prepare the rooms."

The next morning, we were supposed to drive through the Passage of Dry Bones, a merciless mountain passage where accidents were common, especially in bad weather. When we looked outside our hotel window in the morning, thick fog covered the narrow, twisted way leading from the village to the mountains. Our mood plummeted, thinking about what would happen next.

Even Shimon and Keren acknowledged our distress. Shimon suggested giving Noshad a yogurt drink with a strong anesthetic that would make him sleepy. He explained that he could become the new driver, our unexpected savior. Shimon said he was an experienced, trained driver in such mountain passages; before his military service, he participated in a jeep trip to the Golan Heights. When we made more inquiries regarding the subject, it became clear that he had been sitting in the back of the jeep during the entire trip.

Since we had no narcotics in our possession, we decided to talk to Noshad before leaving the hotel. A few minutes before departure, we summoned Noshad for a clarification talk. We explained our unequivocal rules for driving in the mountains. He nodded without uttering a word, rubbed his long mustache, and glanced nervously to the side of the road.

The drive started with a climb over moderate slopes, and Noshad drove carefully. We settled comfortably in our seats. After an hour of calm drive, we saw a sign indicating that we were getting closer to the mountain. When we glanced ahead we saw that blanket of fog and clouds had wrapped the peak like a turban. Noshad started mumbling his mantra, gripping the steering wheel. Odelia and I took a deep breath, trying to prepare ourselves for the new nightmare. Shimon and Keren relaxed behind us, realizing that something extraordinary was about to happen.

We were over thirteen thousand feet now, completely enveloped in fog. The rocky path ahead was no more than twelve feet wide, flanked by a treacherous cliff that was waiting for any minor error in judgment. The fog was so heavy that it was impossible to guess the location of the gorge. Perhaps on the right? Or the left? Or maybe in front of us?

Noshad accelerated. At this stage, only Ganesh, the elephant god, had any impact on this spine-chilling trip. I had kept my final threat for a real emergency. Now was the time to use it.

"If you continue driving like this, we won't pay you the rest of the money," I shouted, but Noshad was not impressed. He was focused on his crazy driving, his eyes fixed forward, lips mumbling the same monotonous prayer. He sliced through the deep fog like a Japanese fighter plane on a suicide mission. From time to time we would see vague flashes of a passing military truck, its lights blinding and its horn deafening. Noshad would turn sharply and we knew we were on the edge of the cliff, hanging by a thread.

Shimon and Keren enjoyed every minute. They adapted a colorful vocabulary to each of our suicidal driver's tricks. Each time Noshad managed to evade the vehicle coming toward us, they would howl, "Faster, *babu*, faster!"

After we had crossed a particularly dangerous passage, they would scream: "Driver number one in India!"

The truly frightening moments happened when Noshad and a truck driver approached each other with screeching brakes. Someone had to back up to clear the way. Noshad would place the jeep in reverse so the other truck could pass through, going back to the edge of the cliff until we could feel that we were starting to slide down. In those special moments, Keren would scream a special motivational phrase: "I love you, *babu!*"

Odelia and I were confined to our seats. Noshad was our ticket to either Manali or to the next world. Miraculously, we crossed the Passage of Dry Bones and started descending to the valley below. The scenery changed from a frozen wasteland to alpine forests, waterfalls, and mountain slopes covered with colorful flowers. The snowy peaks vanished and green replaced the yellow.

Two hours later we arrived in Manali. Odelia and I looked at each other and a huge sense of relief washed over us. We did it! We were alive! We had managed to survive!

We felt like we could kiss Noshad, Ganesh, and any other Indian that crossed our way.

Noshad dropped us by a busy river in the middle of Manali. He leaned over a rock, smoking a stinking cigarette. I unloaded our stuff, then looked at him. What did he think of us? He almost certainly saw us as hysterical Western tourists. When I finished unloading our backpacks, I went to pay him. He took the money and shoved it in his pocket without counting it, nodding his head.

Odelia shook his hand, Shimon patted his shoulders, and Keren hugged him and said with a big smile: "Driver number one in India!" Noshad didn't say anything. He got into his jeep, honked a few times, then drove down the hill.

Strange, but at that moment I was full of appreciation for Noshad. After all, he'd succeeded in his mission and transported us whole to a safe harbor.

I was still deep in thought, but Shimon and Keren did not waste any time. They'd heard about a restaurant in Manali that served *jahnun* (a Yemenite dish) like in Israel and they wanted to check out the place. Odelia and I needed rest. We promised to join Shimon and Keren in an hour. We rented a room in one of the picturesque guest houses in Manali, and Odelia inaugurated the small room by locking herself up in the toilet and throwing up. I too felt a bit wobbly. We covered ourselves with a dirty quilt and fell asleep immediately.

We woke up after twelve hours feeling like shipwreck survivors. When we went to the restaurant, darkness surrounded us. We found a note stuck on a wall:

> *Eyal and Odelia,*
>
> *We waited for a long time; you never showed up. We are off to Dharamshala. It was great traveling with you!*

Love,

Shimon and Keren.

*P.S. Remember who protected us
during all this trip.*

At the bottom of the note was a hand-drawn image of Ganesh, the elephant god, embracing us, the four intrepid travelers, while Noshad smiles widely under Ganesh's trunk.

CHAPTER SIX

THE TOWER OF BABEL

AT A CASUAL BACKPACKER CAFÉ in Dharamshala, India, we met a young British couple that aroused our curiosity. Aurelio was a British citizen of Spanish origin, a descendant of a respectable family from Toledo, Spain. With his sleepy brown eyes, scruffy beard, and long black hair tied up with a colorful rubber band, he had the air of someone who has seen it all. Caroline was hiding behind a disheveled wild mane and thick-rimmed spectacles. Occasionally, her blue eyes would flicker with a skittish glitter, but usually she let Aurelio do the talking.

This young couple suffered from chronic fatigue coupled with extreme disgust for any kind of physical activity, including even the easiest nature stroll. They had refined lazy lounging in coffee shops to an art form. In the early afternoon hours, after a long, sweet sleep, they would show up in the café, grab a strategic table that looked over the dusty street, then spend the entire day there without moving. They usually stayed put until the late-night hours or till the last guest left the café.

During all those long hours, they played card games with complicated rules that dragged on for hours on end, wrote long letters to all the people they had met in the past, and chain-smoked while staring at the old wooden ceiling fan overhead.

Aurelio had a special Zippo cigarette lighter that was handed down through the generations from one family member to another. It was engraved with the initials of his grandfather, who had fought in the first World War and had never let go of the lighter even at the toughest moments. Aurelio invested hours on end in the family lighter. He developed an entire world of content around it. Every day he took it apart and cleaned it before putting it back together with the most meticulous attention. Anyone who showed the slightest interest earned the right to hear the glorious family history of the Alejandro family from their cheerful Toledo days and learn that Aurelio's great-grandfather used to roll cigarettes with specially prepared tobacco and light it with this very same lighter.

Although Aurelio and Caroline only wandered from one coffee shop to another, they gathered quite a lot of useful information by conversing with backpackers all day long, week after week. In a way, they worked like secret agents, listening carefully to everything that was said to them—including conversations at nearby tables— taking meticulous notes of everything they heard. They entered their observations in thick, worn-out notebooks, cross-referencing new information against prior information. The result was that they had the most updated, exhaustive information available. Even though they had never visited most of the destinations they kept notes about, they could tell you everything you needed to know, from the mundane, such as visa requirements, to the exotic, such as who you need to bribe if you get in trouble in Indonesia.

Backpackers used to gather around their table and drink their advice thirstily, knowing that they were getting the most reliable, updated information. Anyone who needed to know something would approach them, and they would answer patiently, spicing their advice with anecdotes and jokes.

The owners of the coffee shops Aurelio and Caroline visited were astonished at the stream of guests that came to worship these Western oracles. Within a few days they'd won special status: the coffee shops' owners did not charge them for food or drink. In fact, Aurelio and Caroline became so famous that oftentimes it was enough to quote them to determine significant issues. For instance, if five backpackers were arguing about the cheapest way to get from Hanoi to Saigon, the magic phrase "Aurelio said that . . ." would handily bring the argument to a close.

As our next stop after India was Singapore, we decided to get the best advice directly from the source. The minute we mentioned our plans, Aurelio pulled out another cigarette and lit it nervously with his famous Zippo lighter, saying nothing. Caroline disappeared into her hair. After he had finished smoking, Aurelio seemed much calmer. He sat back comfortably in the chair that had been his fixed spot for the last eight hours and started talking about his own experience in Singapore.

To our surprise, before becoming a wanderer, Aurelio had had a career as a software developer. When he and Caroline arrived in Singapore, they fell in love with the city but were alarmed at the high cost of living. They decided to find a stable source of income so they could stay longer. Aurelio got a haircut, bought a new suit from a local tailor at a bargain price, shoved his Zippo lighter deep into an inside pocket, and went out to look for a job. He was lucky: one of the big banks was looking for a software developer that would work with clients in South America. Aurelio, who spoke Spanish and English fluently, was an ideal candidate.

The beginning was promising. Aurelio bloomed in his first real job. His fellow workers loved to hear about his adventures, his managers liked his professionalism. Aurelio and Caroline were enchanted by the exemplary tidiness of their new city, and fell in love with the technological efficiency that was evident everywhere. After three months, Aurelio decided to let his hair grow back—a harmless decision that led to disastrous results. The managers who had consulted with him in the past about tech trends started to ignore his advice. His fellow workers who used to enjoy his stories about faraway lands began to distance themselves in case the tag of a rebel would stick to them as well. The noose tightened as his hair grew longer. Aurelio was now eating alone in the company cafeteria, drinking coffee in dark spots, sneaking silently from one floor to the other.

When the pressure became unbearable, he resigned, and he and Caroline left Singapore.

Despite this unpleasant experience, they supplied us with intel. The main problem in Singapore, they warned us, was hotel rates. The magic phrase we learned from them was *Bencoolen Street*. According to Aurelio, there was one building on this street where we could avoid the crazy prices. The building was slated for demolition but still being used for temporary housing and dormitories. When we asked about the living conditions there, he lit another cigarette with his Zippo and vanished behind a thick cloud of smoke.

When Odelia and I arrived at the Singapore Changi Airport, every label of obsessive efficiency attached to this city was justified. Our suitcases arrived at the conveyor belt in no time. The city itself was polished to a shine. We tried our luck in a few hotels, but the closer we got to the city center, the more our panic increased at the high prices. Singapore was the first Western city we'd arrived at after six months of traveling in India and Nepal, so the insane rates were a shock. One night in a hotel was equal to a two-week journey in India or Nepal. We were determined not to fall into the trap, but as we investigated further, our resolve weakened. Totally worn out, we pulled out the notebook with Aurelio and Caroline's tips. We asked a Singaporean on the street how to get to this building on Bencoolen Street. He looked at us with astonishment, saying this was not a place for people like us. But we did not give in, and eventually we found our way there.

Our building was locked between new high-rises, sticking out like a sore thumb. As an omen, our "hotel" did not have a name or sign. Aurelio's words echoed in my ear: "The bus will drop you five hundred meters from the place. You should cross the street to the other side, pass two construction sites, then you will see the building on your right. The entrance is through a long, narrow tunnel. Take the elevator up to the third floor. Once you get there, ask for Mustafa."

We followed his instructions to the letter. The first construction site was covered with construction waste. The second site was a high-rise residential building, partly destroyed. A wrecking ball rolled over our heads in a stretched-out arch, tearing down gigantic pieces of the building. Whenever it hit the building, huge chunks of cement dropped down like breadcrumbs from a giant's beard. The noise was unbearable and a cloud of dust covered the place in a suffocating blanket.

Adjacent to the site we saw a tunnel covered with green tarp. Coughing from the dust, we rushed into it and followed its long twists until we were discharged in front of a ramshackle building. Black garbage cans created an obstacle course that led to the entrance. The exterior had long since been peeled off, exposing iron girders that peeped out of the building's shell.

The entrance was dark. Narrow stairs led us to the mezzanine, where the sharp smell of heavily spiced food filled the air. One fluorescent bulb out of three was lit, flickering weakly, as if asking for help. A piece of cardboard stuck above the elevator announced that reception was on the third floor. We pressed the elevator button. A few moments later the elevator door opened and several people came out. Not one of them looked like a backpacker or a tourist.

We arrived at the third floor and found ourselves in a dimly lit corridor. We walked ahead till we found ourselves in an open area. In one corner several women were nursing their babies. In another corner, a tall, skinny guy with a yellow turban was stirring a large pot on a gas stove. The strong aroma of spiced meat filled the room. It dawned on us that we had come to a very strange place. It was not quite a hostel; it seemed that people were calling this shabby building home. When we asked about Mustafa, one of the women pointed forward.

A small sign over a nook in the wall told us this was the reception office. A metal bell with a golden patina rested on a worn-out wooden counter. We rang the bell, but no one showed up. A woman passed through the corridor, so we asked again where we could find Mustafa. She pointed at the floor and moved on. We did not get her point. Was she insinuating a secret door beneath the reception desk, or perhaps an underground tunnel that would lead us to the mysterious Mustafa?

We stood, lost, at the counter. After a few minutes, the woman returned, took Odelia's hand, and ushered her around the counter, pointing down. Under the counter we found Mustafa in the flesh, sleeping peacefully on a wooden stool. It was twelve noon.

I shook his shoulders several times until he opened his eyes. He was about forty, unshaven, dark-skinned, with a charming smile. After getting up, he combed back his thin hair and shared with us that he was the one running the place on behalf of a wealthy Chinese family. We nodded to show our appreciation. The rate was ten dollars a day, including a continental breakfast. He stroked his tummy to emphasize how worthwhile it would be to wait for such a meal.

It looked like a no-brainer. A room for ten dollars a day, at a central location, including breakfast! Excited, we thanked him for the excellent deal. Mustafa smiled graciously. He said that almost all the beds were occupied, but he was sure we could find two vacant beds. He handed us a small blue card with our names and the date we arrived at the institution.

We set out to find two available beds. The building was amazingly packed. The narrow corridors had been converted into a labyrinth of tiny rooms with thin plaster walls. Every vacant inch was used to squeeze in more people. We started our tour on the fourth floor. It was occupied by Thai people and had no vacant beds. On the fifth floor we found only Ghanaians. By the time we reached the sixth floor we understood how it worked: every floor was devoted to a specific nationality. The sixth floor had Pakistanis, the eighth floor Chinese, the ninth floor Indians. We did not try the seventh, because Mustafa said it was full. He said that quickly, as if fearing we would ask more questions.

The eighth floor was taken by Chinese nationals, also full. We climbed up to the ninth floor. The smell there was indescribable, a scent that reminded us of the calming effect of the ocean. When we reached the dormitory area, we saw a short Indian man frying sardines in their original tin over a small camping stove. The sardines sizzled in the boiling oil as he flipped them from side to side, smiling contently.

We introduced ourselves.

The amateur chef's name was Raju. He had been staying there for six months and seemed fully adjusted to the place. Rows of three-level bunk beds were arranged along the walls. Two beds opposite one another had no blue stickers over them, so this was our lucky floor. The beds had thin, yellowish sponge mattresses tossed on a net of rusty springs. If mattresses could talk, I am sure they could fill entire volumes with stories about the characters who had lain down on them. My mattress had battle scars: a huge hole at the top that looked like the result of a shark attack, and black spray-paint at the bottom, probably to hide something awful. There was no ladder or step to ease the climb to the upper bunks.

A slanted window overlooked the noisy street below. Several panes were shattered, which added to the authentic charm of the place. Occasional throbbing shook the entire building; when we looked outside, we saw the giant metal ball wreaking havoc next door. The general atmosphere reminded us of a prison that had deteriorated into such poor condition that even the wardens had decided to leave, letting the prisoners determine their own fate.

It is amazing to see how fast a person can adjust to a new situation. A few hours had passed, and we already felt that we belonged there. We left our backpacks on our beds and headed out for a walk in our neighborhood.

Within minutes we were on a shiny main street with plenty of prestigious stores and fancy restaurants, a far cry from our shabby lodging. Time passed quickly. By the evening we decided to go back to the hotel. In the elevator we bumped into two bearded muscular guys wearing tight black undershirts and wide black rapper pants striped in grey. They did not speak, but their piercing black eyes felt like heavy weights on us. They exited the elevator on the seventh floor, the floor Mustafa skipped in our grand tour. When we arrived at our floor, we asked Raju about the tenants on the seventh floor.

"These are the Iranians," Raju explained with a smile. He did not look disturbed by their menacing presence. "They refuse to accept anyone else to their floor. No one knows what they are up to. I believe that they do two things in there: pray and lift weights."

The codes in the building were taken from penal institutions anywhere in the world. The Thai floor was designated the white-collar section. At night, they smoked cheap cigarettes, wearing shiny shorts, worn-out undershirts, and black flip-flops. In the morning everything changed. Sunlight transformed those shady characters of the night into respectable bank clerks wearing ties, exemplary citizens who had left their gloomy existence behind them.

The role of the wardens was taken by the "ayatollahs of the East." No one dared to mess with them as they wandered around the building like watchful tigers, waiting for a confrontation that would make them demonstrate their power over us.

Mustafa proved to be a local magician who knew everybody and could arrange for you anything you liked, from mosquito repellent to a job with a construction company. He was liked by tenants of all nationalities from all floors. In time I wondered what the secret of his charm was. I think the main reason for his success was the fact that he cared about us, helping anyone he met without expecting any compensation. He'd patiently waited while we looked for our beds, given us excellent info about Singapore, loaned us an umbrella on a rainy day. Everything he did was with a genuine smile and intimate understanding of the human soul. He acted like the Secretary General of the United Nations of this building, the glue that held the tenants of this Singaporean Tower of Babel together.

Every morning we gathered for breakfast on the fifth floor. The prestigious meal included a tepid cup of tea, a thin sausage wedged into a dry bun, and sweetened raspberry juice in a small orange plastic cup, all served on a metal tray. The kitchen manager was an older Chinese lady who managed the place with an iron fist. While we waited in line, she stared at each person poignantly, trying to determine whether we were real guests in this fine establishment who had the right to receive this bountiful meal or we had sneaked in from the other side of the island. After a tense moment, she would nod at us, signaling that we could move forward, then set the food on our trays with a suspicious look, as if not fully trusting her instincts. Odelia used to skip this meal, but I was quite interested in the diversity of characters who gathered from all the floors for this breakfast. We would sit in silence, focusing on the sausage, dreaming about the life outside, looking around to see what kind of food the other prisoners had gotten.

One morning, an energetic British lady joined us for breakfast. Judy was about seventy years old, with blue eyes and mop of white hair. On her tray, beside the sausage, she had a sweet red apple. We all stared at the apple in disbelief, thinking the same thing—how on earth had she succeeded in getting an apple from the kitchen?

"She must have had exemplary behavior in this prison," I told the Malaysian man beside me. A wave of laughter rose around the table. The Malaysian roared with laughter, holding his tummy as if he had just heard the funniest joke in the world. The next day I woke up early as usual to get to breakfast on time. At the entrance to the dining room I felt that something had changed. The Chinese lady was standing by the stainless-steel trays, holding a large ladle, faking a thin smile. To my surprise, we received porridge in addition to the regular meal. Any time the lady drew a boiling spoon of porridge and thrust it onto a tray, her mouth twisted in a forced smile.

Mustafa passed between the tables, exchanging jokes with the inmates, tapping a new detainee on the shoulder, exchanging a few sentences about the weather with Judy. The international world of diplomacy was missing a star, no question about that. He sat at the end of the table, and when he was sure he had everybody's attention, he started to talk.

"We've received a warning from the Singapore health department that this building doesn't meet basic sanitary conditions."

He stopped there and looked at us, making sure we understood the gravity of this news. When he was satisfied that he had our full attention, he continued. "On Monday morning supervisors from the Health and

Sanitation Office will visit to decide whether the place may stay open. We need help in cleaning up everything. To encourage you to help, we decided that those who volunteer for the mission will get a free week of stay in the building."

All the permanent tenants volunteered for the clean-up mission. Most of the tenants could not afford to move anywhere else, so the possibility of shutting down the building was an existential threat to them. I raised my hand as well, thinking that this would be an experience to remember. To my surprise, Judy took on the challenge as well.

The next day we all reported to the third floor to receive instructions and cleaning supplies. A tropical rain was pouring outside, but inside the building a solid collection of nationalities, one that would make any foreign legion officer happy, gathered.

The collection of characters that showed up for this battle was determined not to fail. For them, this was a battle against the city, an opportunity to redeem themselves, to work out their feelings of discrimination, of being treated like cheap foreign labor left behind in Singapore's crazy race to progress.

Mustafa examined us carefully. This was not the Mustafa we had known. He looked taller, stronger, more noble. He nodded contentedly, but like every good commander, Mustafa knew that a motivational speech was needed to secure success.

"I've been living here for almost twelve years," said Mustafa in quiet voice. "I've seen a lot during these years." His voice trailed off as he made a show of remembering some of the things that he witnessed here. He then raised his voice a bit. "This is not the first time they've tried to chase us out of here. They wish to turn this building into a fancy tower. They want us out of the city. They want us to leave Singapore!"

The legion uttered sounds of protest.

Mustafa's voice rose louder. "We are considered negative elements. Can you believe it?" He scanned the ragtag gang before him with an astonished look, raising his left hand in a solemn vow. His voice became hoarse with excitement.

"I'm telling you: I'm not moving from here! If they want to chase us out, they will need to physically remove us from our home, and I'm not going to give them the pleasure!"

The legion uttered roars of content. "We won't give up!" someone shouted from the back. A somber Pakistani next to me cried, "We will show them who's the boss here!"

Mustafa nodded in satisfaction. We each collected our cleaning supplies: detergents, rags, and mops. A surprising addition was a set of new pink sheets. Apparently, the thinking was that new bedclothes would provide uniformity while hiding the hideous mattresses. The sheets were not soft or indulgent, but rather thin and scratchy. When we started walking through the floors, holding our new sheets in two outstretched hands, we must have looked like new prisoners walking toward our cells, getting a noisy reception from the other inmates.

Mustafa divided us into teams, and each team received a floor of its own. In a brilliant move, he'd decided not to let tenants clean their own floor. He knew very well that this would allow him to get rid of the junk that had accumulated in the prison. The instructions were simple: throw away everything that could be considered junk, clean everything that could not be removed. We were ordered to put all our personal belongings on the bed so they would not be discarded by mistake. The atmosphere among the prisoners was jolly. It was a kind of holiday from ordinary life, an opportunity to break the strict codes.

My five-person team's mission was to clean the Iranians' floor. Duration: two hours. I was with Raju, a young Nigerian, Judy, and a skinny Pakistani. We crammed into the elevator and Raju pressed the button. When the elevator opened, we stepped hesitantly into a narrow corridor that was decorated with framed pictures of weightlifters and American rappers. We looked back to make sure no one was following us. Heavy weights were all over the place. A long mirror hung opposite the entrance. Rolled gym mats were on one side, and on the wall ahead were oversized photos of Ayatollah Khomeini and Arnold Schwarzenegger as Conan the Barbarian. A massive stationary punching bag blocked the exit to the stairs. Mustafa had said very clearly that all exits must be free of obstacles as per fire department regulations. Raju and the Pakistani tried to move the bag, but after several minutes of strained groaning they signaled to us for help.

After several attempts we decided to turn the bag on its side so we could roll it away from the emergency exit. As we turned the bag, it fell to the floor and the neck of the stand broke. Something hit the floor with a metallic clunk. Judy picked it up before passing it around; it was a shiny new Rolex.

"An excellent forgery," said Raju, emerging as a watch enthusiast. "Only an expert will be able to tell the difference. They probably sell each watch for five hundred dollars." When we looked inside the bag, we counted eleven watches. None of us wanted to get in trouble with the crazy Iranians, and only one person could help us solve this issue. Judy was sent to look for Mustafa.

He came quickly, taking the Rolex from Raju, who was still impressed by the perfect forgery. Mustafa weighed the watch in his hand, considering the options. His hand closed on it and he looked at all of us with a serious expression. He coughed several times before addressing us in an encouraging voice.

"It's not your fault."

We all breathed a bit easier. He nodded in understanding, then added, "But if they find out you know about their business, you will be in trouble."

The team showed signs of anxiety. Mustafa continued to work the audience. "Believe me, you don't want to mess with them. They don't have any sense of humor about their business." He paused, pointing at Ayatollah Khomeini, who was watching the scene sternly.

Mustafa approached the bag, pulled out four watches, and distributed them among us. He gave Raju the watch he was holding. Raju looked happy; it was clear he was not aware of the trouble we were in.

"Hide them well. Don't wear them until you leave this place. I will tell them that I have cut a deal with you. They do not know who you are. Trust me, I will not give you up. If there is any trouble, they will come to me. What happened here will be erased from everyone's memory the minute I leave this room. Is that clear?"

The watch burned in my pocket as I nodded.

When we all met on the fifth floor again, the consensus was that the building was ready for inspection. The Iranians were nowhere to be seen. I wondered if they were gathering to plan what to do with our bodies. Mustafa shook our hands, and I almost saluted him when he passed me. He reminded us to behave like exemplary citizens during the inspection.

The next day, the day of the inspection, Odelia and I had an excellent lunch at a noisy, crowded Chinese restaurant before returning to our floor. In the corridor we were welcomed by the same intoxicating summer scent that reminded us of Jaffa Port in Israel. Raju was frying sardines again. I told him that if he wanted to go on living in this building, he should stop cooking immediately. Even after he got rid of his sardines, the smell was still extraordinarily strong. In desperation, Odelia pulled out her CK perfume and sprayed the room to mask the smell.

How can I describe the combination of perfume and fried sardines? Nevertheless, there was something attractive about this new fragrance. I started considering a brand name for it, something like "A Scent from the Abyss."

We heard Mustafa in the narrow corridor explaining to the supervisors that the air conditioning was not working this morning. The group entered our room in a firm step. We greeted the two supervisors—a tall and a short guy, both with thin mustaches—and Mustafa, who was trying to look indifferent. The short supervisor sniffed the air.

"What's this smell?"

Mustafa started to stammer. It was the first time we'd ever seen him like that. He mumbled something about the proximity to the ocean, as if that shabby building were a beach house open to the healing sea air. He looked trapped. I wondered if he would pull two watches out of his pocket to try to close another shady deal.

The short supervisor inhaled deeply, then smiled, nodding in approval. "This is a good smell. Reminds me of the fresh fish my wife buys at the market on Sundays."

He continued to sniff the air, his forehead wrinkled in concentration.

The next day, Mustafa broke the news to us: we'd passed the test. All week long we received little surprises at breakfast: an apple, a mango, fresh hot cookies. A week later we were back to the prison routine. The pink sheets became floor cloths, Raju resumed frying sardines on the camp stove, and whenever I was in the elevator with one of the Iranian weightlifters, I had an inexplicable urge to confess everything.

During the next couple of weeks, I tried desperately to acquire plane tickets to Australia. I was exhausted from the stress and noticed that my fellow Operation Iran team members did not look recovered, either. The Nigerian and the Pakistani vanished, despite the free week promised to everyone who helped. Judy told me that she was not afraid, but two days later, she disappeared in the middle of the night. Raju and I were the last ones left from the original team.

Multiple attempts to acquire cheap tickets ended in disappointment, and we could not afford to pay full price. I started thinking that we would never get out of Singapore. Odelia decided to turn to Mustafa for help.

Within a few hours, two cheap tickets to Australia appeared from nowhere. I stared at the tickets and the suffocating feeling I'd had for a while evaporated. I started humming the song "Freedom" by Aretha Franklin. Raju

looked at me, surprised. He did not seem to have been
affected by the Iranian affair at all.

On the day we left, we woke up Mustafa, who was
sleeping under the counter. We thanked him for everything, hugged him, and returned the blue plastic cards he
gave us on the day we arrived. When we boarded the bus
to the airport, I glanced for the last time at our beloved
building. The neighboring building looked as if it was
going to collapse any minute. I wondered when our building would meet the same fate.

After we left the city, the watch stopped burning in my
pocket. I wore it on my wrist. It looked like a piece of art,
but the discrepancy between the prestige it reflected and
my sloppy appearance was too extreme. I put it back in
my backpack and there it stayed till the end of the trip.

Today, the watch is left in a bottom drawer at home.
The passing of time has not been favorable to it. It
stopped working and the frame rusted, turning it into
a cheap flea-market gift. Occasionally, we take it out and
pass it from one to the other, remembering the adventure we had with the colorful foreign legion that had
gathered together in that ramshackle building, and managed in stopping, against all odds but only temporarily,
Singapore's aggressive journey toward progress.

CHAPTER SEVEN

PLAYING CHICKEN

AFTER VISITING THE TWO MAIN cities in Australia, Melbourne and Sidney, and taking an unforgettable trip along the coast between those two beautiful cities, we decided it was time for the real thing: the huge drylands called the Outback that cover most of the enormous subcontinent, far from the soothing presence of the ocean.

Our journey to the endless Outback started in the city of Adelaide, right on the shores of the Indian Ocean. From there, we took an eight-hour bus ride to the edge of the Australian desert that ended in Broken Hill, New South Wales. This forsaken town is the gateway to the local version of the American Wild West. The landscape is arid, unforgiving, and characterized by big open sky, low bushes, and an eerie calm.

Broken Hill was established during the Australian gold rush by a strange group of visionaries, adventurers, and gold seekers. Years passed, the mines shut down, and now it feels like a ghost town whose inhabitants have not yet accepted their dreary status. The digging machines are rusty monuments stationed around the town like grotesque tombstones, and the ever-present dust covers the houses in a thin layer of longing for their glorious past. It's one of those places where anyone who could leave did so without regret, and those who stayed against all odds developed a deep local pride expressed as bitter resentment when anyone dares to insinuate that this abandoned place belongs to the distant past.

Broken Hill gets a few moments of glory when filming crews select it for shooting apocalyptic desert scenes. Then the town becomes a place that reflects the evasive sense of the huge Australian wasteland, with roads stretching to infinity, dry bushes swirling in the hot wind, big lizards warming up in the beating sun. Here they shot *Mad Max: The Road Warrior*, where Max drives across the postapocalyptic landscape of the Australian Outback, trying to survive in a barren land against barbarian bandits.

Tired from the long journey and without an ounce of patience for a drawn-out search for appropriate accommodations, we decided to enter the first hostel we saw. After a few minutes of walking in the merciless sun, we saw a shabby building that looked like a hostel. A large sign above the entrance had "Do Not Break the House Rules" written in large red letters. We entered the dimly lit hallway, and there we found Doug, the colorful proprietor of this fine establishment—or as we soon would call him, Doug the Road Warrior. He was about sixty years old, of average height, plump, and unshaven, with thinning grey hair. He wore shabby grey pants and a faded under-shirt. He was limping on his left leg and relied on an impressive walking stick made from a dense ebony wood. The walking stick bore strange carvings and its head was a worn copper knob. Doug's eyes twitched nervously; he resembled a minor character in an early Clint Eastwood Western. Maybe the cunning bartender who always man-aged to survive the awful shooting incident that took place at the only inn in town.

But Doug was not keen on playing a supporting role. Soon enough, we found out that he'd promoted himself to the role of the local sheriff, which he performed with such enthusiasm that it seemed as if Hollywood had lost a budding star, a gifted actor who was wasting his talent in Australia's desolate Outback.

When we first met Doug, we couldn't have guessed that our short stay in his sleepy town would end in a dra-matic confrontation—a duel that any Hollywood director would be happy to shoot under the bright blue sky of Broken Hill.

After we checked in, writing our personal details in a large notebook under Doug's suspicious eye, he ushered us to our room. He limped slowly in his gloomy kingdom, knocking on the battered floors with his walking stick. After a few twists, we reached the kitchen through a pair of wooden saloon doors. This was a surprisingly large room adorned with an old green braided rug and signs of various sizes.

Doug started talking, waving his stick to stress various points, but we were focused on the signs. There were so many of them, all phrased in the same threatening style. The sign on the fridge said "We will use all means possible against anyone who is caught stealing someone else's food."

I wondered what "all means" meant, but my attention was already caught up by a larger sign:

"Checkout is at 9 a.m. Whoever fails to evacuate his room in time will bear the consequences."

Another sign hung from two rusty hooks and swayed from side to side, as if alluding at the fate of the trespasser:

"Theft of any kind will not be tolerated in Broken Hill. Anyone who steals plates, cutlery, or cups will be punished."

There were no mentions of specific penalties or what punishment would look like, but the vague threats had a chilling effect. The warnings were a masterpiece of intimidation. Doug continued to explain the exact process for washing the dishes:

"Right after you finish eating, you must wash the dishes with the yellow sponge, then dry each piece of tableware separately with the white towel." He waved a filthy towel of an unidentified color in our faces. "Then put it back in the cupboard, exactly in the spot it was taken from."

He scanned us carefully before he continued. "This is important to me when I show the place to newcomers. Is that clear?"

We nodded, exhausted. After the long bus ride, all we could think of was the comfortable bed waiting for us, but Doug went on, using the same hoarse, threatening tone. He provided examples of wrong behavior, spicing his words with a list of vague punishments that awaited whoever dared to violate the house rules. He emphasized that if you violated even one rule, there was no way back.

At long last, he relented and showed us to our room. The tiny space had two single beds on either side of an old chest whose legs were linked by a rusty iron chain to a plastic wastebasket, apparently to prevent someone from running off with the wastebasket or the chest and starting a new life elsewhere. An exposed lamp cast pale light on the bare walls. The room was stifling, as there was no breeze coming through its single tiny window that faced a wire fence.

After a brief, troubled nap, we stepped out of the room, looking for the showers. A bright sign welcomed us:

"Broken Hill suffers from water shortages. The showers are operated with quarters and are limited to one minute per person!"

We took the fastest shower of our lives, then went out to buy food for dinner and returned to the large kitchen area, where we encountered the other lost souls that had found their way to Doug's kingdom. We quickly estimated that there were ten more guests in the hostel. In all the other places we'd stayed, the kitchen was always messy and noisy. One often had to shout to be heard. Doug's kitchen enjoyed an eerie kind of silence. Everyone was cooking silently, arguing in hushed voices about the privilege of doing the dishes. The most fearful types allowed their food to become cold while they washed, dried, and put back the dishes they had used.

The travelers looked like children at a strict boarding school, waiting for someone to slip, to break one of the rules. The air was heavy with anxiety. Doug constantly walked amongst the guests, casting a menacing presence, mumbling things no one could understand, opening random cupboards to check see if the dishes inside were clean and dry. Whenever he opened a cupboard to see if the dishes were back in place, we all said a prayer.

The evening passed pleasantly. Miraculously, the place emptied around nine thirty; Odelia and I were the only guests left in the kitchen, watching a fashion show on the kitchen television. A sign above the television informed us in no uncertain terms that "You may watch till 10 p.m."

A big round clock next to the sign left no room for any misunderstanding. Doug continued to patrol outside, stepping through the squeaking wooden door occasionally to see if we were still there.

The closer the clock's hands moved to ten o'clock, the darker his gaze became. When the clock read five minutes to ten, Doug stood behind us, motionless, his stare burning our backs. I told Odelia that I valued my life and would not risk it for a fashion show. Odelia answered coolly that we had five more minutes. I tried to talk her out of it, but she insisted on staying to watch the show until the deadline. I knew that when she was in that mood, anything I said was pointless.

Time passed like an old man climbing a steep hill. Doug stood there, unmoving, waiting for a violation that would allow him to act. When the clock showed two minutes to ten, I turned toward him. Doug smiled, but it was not a soothing smile. His twisted grin resembled the look of a sadistic prison guard that had managed to trap a poor inmate. *In a few moments,* said Doug's smile, *I will dish out my punishment.*

The hostel was quiet. No one was around. I imagined the headline of the morning newspaper: "Backpackers Beaten to Death at Doug's Hostel After Violating Law #15 Forbidding Watching Television After 10 P.M."

Reading this headline, I gathered, the good people of Broken Hill would click their tongues and say, "Poor souls, but oh, they did deserve it. After all, there was a specific warning, wasn't there?"

At 10:00 P.M. sharp, Odelia rose from the couch to turn off the television. I examined Doug's face. He was focused on Odelia, his bloodshot eyes expressing what he could not utter aloud, his tongue licking his lower lip. Odelia was not impressed and bade him an indifferent "good night." His ominous stare followed us to the end of the corridor.

The confrontation was avoided for the time being, but I had no doubt the power struggle would continue the next day. Both parties had uttered the battle cry; it was a matter of time until these two great powers collided. The desolation of Australia's Outback was mirrored in Doug's eyes as a gathering storm. There was no doubt that he would look for the next opportunity to strike.

After a brief discussion that night, Odelia and I decided to leave Broken Hill the next day and take the bus to Sydney, a journey of fifteen hours. I was ready to travel forty hours to get away from this nutcase and his rule-infested kingdom.

Despite the decision to leave the next day, I went to sleep quite troubled. Odelia fell asleep fast, but I kept turning restlessly, imagining all kinds of scenarios in my busy mind, one chasing another at nightmarish speed. The only bus in this deserted town would arrive in early afternoon. What would happen until then? I'd seen the look on Doug's face. He was defeated once, but he would not let Odelia have the upper hand again.

Loud cries and scary bangs woke me up from the horrid dream that engulfed me. I managed to recognize Doug's voice through the fog of waking up. "It's eight a.m.," he roared. "You have one hour left to vacate the room!" He delivered a frightful blow to everyone's door, but I could have sworn he knocked on ours more violently.

At nine sharp we evacuated the room and took our luggage down to the kitchen. I approached Doug with a shaking voice to ask if we could stay at the hostel till noon. To my great surprise, he exposed his yellowish teeth in a failed attempt to smile and said we should feel right at home. His eyes were glittering with inexplicable excitement at this last chance to regain his honor. I swore to myself I would not give him any reason for confrontation.

The morning passed slowly without event. The distress I had felt left me. We had breakfast, exchanging travel stories with the other backpackers who'd found refuge from the merciless sun in the cool kitchen. Doug was there all the time, somewhere in the background, circling us like a hungry shark waiting for a second of distraction to attack.

When we finished eating, I washed the dishes thoroughly, scrubbing each plate and glass stubbornly, determined not to make a mistake. Someone called Doug outside and he limped hurriedly through the wooden swinging doors. At that minute I heard Odelia calling me to watch a television show with her about New Zealand, our next stop.

I left the sink to join Odelia, who was watching the show while leafing through a magazine. The TV screen showed emerald-green lakes, huge icebergs, wild beaches. Everything seemed so green, far from the grey desert that was breathing heavily around us under the beating Australian sun.

We jumped up at the sound of a fierce cry. Turning around, we saw Doug, his face red, neck veins swollen, beating his stick on a pile of clean dishes submerged in a small puddle of water. Two Japanese travelers stood by his side with their backpacks on, looking totally shocked. Doug's words came to me as if passing through a powerful filter:

"Who didn't dry and put the dishes back in place?"

I froze in my seat. How could I forget to dry and return the dishes to the cupboard? Everyone in the room looked down. Doug's question hovered in the air, hovering over each of our heads as if to determine whom to punish. I glanced at him quickly; his stick fluttered in the air, drawing pictures of subdued violence that could paint any moment with fury. His lips were tightened forcefully, the words hardly coming out, trickling slowly through his clenched mouth.

"For the last time, who didn't return the dishes to their place?"

I prayed that Odelia would not come out to take the blame just to prove a point. She could do it, as under her calm appearance a fearless warrior was hiding, equipped with weapons that could shock any enemy. She did not use this power often; only when she felt threatened or sensed injustice. When she attacked, her eyes would turn into opaque glass, her voice cold. At that moment she could say anything to anyone. I usually admired her for that, but this time I begged her in my heart not to say anything to this nut-head.

A cough from my wife's throat signaled that the duel was about to begin. Odelia folded the magazine and placed it on the table. Her eyes were cold when she addressed Doug in a voice devoid of emotion. "I did not return the dishes to the cabinet."

Doug waved his walking stick in a furious gesture, creating a whooshing sound. Odelia continued to look straight at him, and he looked down for a moment. He had not expected such self-control. He pulled up his trousers, straightened his hair, fondled the engravings on his walking stick.

Suddenly, out of the blue, he roared, "It's against the rules!"

Odelia stepped back a little. Doug's cunning eyes glittered triumphantly. Odelia paled a bit but stood her ground. Her voice was stable when she said, "Since no punishment is specified, could you please tell me how you are going to punish me?"

Doug rolled his eyes, scratched his left ear with a hairy finger, and pulled up his pants while stroking his thinning hair. He tried to say something, but the words stuck in his throat. He coughed coarsely, then stared at Odelia for a moment before lowering his gaze.

Odelia looked around at the astonished faces in the room, then said in the same indifferent tone, "So I assume the case is closed."

Doug did not answer. He turned away and walked through the saloon doors, leaving behind a faint smell of sweat. I approached Odelia and hugged her with an enormous sense of relief. Appreciative stares from backpackers met us on all sides.

Shortly after this confrontation, we boarded the bus that would drop us in Sydney fifteen hours later. The driver was smoking a cigarette outside, and from the window I saw Doug approach the driver with an expression of urgency. He addressed him excitedly, pointing at the bus several times with his walking stick.

"What the hell does he want now?" I asked Odelia.

"To face a firing squad," my wife answered calmly, leafing through the same magazine she'd read before. The driver nodded gravely, looking at the bus. Had Doug asked him to hold us accountable? Did he tell him about the afternoon's mighty battle in which a sacred rule had been broken?

We will never know. A few moments later, the driver got on the bus. Without looking at us, he took the wheel and drove away from the small bus stop in Broken Hill. Through the dark windows of the Greyhound bus, we saw Doug standing in the cloud of dust like a mighty rock, a remnant of another generation that had not been able to adapt to the modern world. I am sure he felt he should have been born at the beginning of the century, when he could have enforced his strict laws without fear of retribution.

As we drove away, Doug's ebony walking stick continued to draw complicated designs in the dust cloud that engulfed him, expressing his deep desires, challenging Odelia to another duel that would end differently, an opportunity to redeem his honor as the self-appointed sheriff of Broken Hill.

CHAPTER EIGHT

WHALES IN KAIKŌURA

WE WAITED FOR THIS ADVENTURE throughout our entire time in New Zealand. "Kaikōura," we whispered during starry nights. "Kaikōura," the word resting on the tongue like fresh cream. "Kaikōura," we addressed one another happily. We'd heard so many stories about the whaling town of Kaikōura, where one could watch sperm whales from a short distance. "Imagine," the travelers returning from there told us, "that you are twenty feet away from a whale that weighs fifty tons, a leviathan of the deep surrounded by dolphins, seals, and sharks."

We listened to those stories with open mouths. Every traveler who came back from there added another amazing detail. One described the shape of the whale's tail; another talked about the excitement of spotting a sperm whale in the wild; yet another talked about the amazing views of the Kaikōura Peninsula flanked by snowcapped mountains. These stories made us so excited that we considered renting a kayak immediately and paddling there ourselves.

Kaikōura is a quiet fishing town on the eastern side of New Zealand's southern island. Alpine mountains on the continental side of the Kaikōura Peninsula create a dramatic vista of blue ocean against snowcapped mountains. Hot and cold ocean currents meeting at the peninsula and deep underwater canyons a short distance from shore bring a dizzying array of marine life to the surface. Underwater mammals know how to recognize a good deal—a quarter of the world's seventy-six existing whale and dolphin species can be found opposite the Kaikōura seashores enjoying what marine biologists call a free-for-all buffet.

Kaikōura has a tumultuous past as a center of whale hunting, but today the Whale Watch Kaikōura company specializes in taking fascinated tourists around the peninsula with the guarantee that ninety percent of the passengers will spot a whale. The earliest tours apparently had the best chances, so there we were at four a.m., waiting for our captain in the lobby, staring with awe at framed photos of giant whales breaching, their huge tails making massive splashes in the water.

Among the many characters wandering around the lobby at that impossible hour, four old women who looked as if they had stepped out of an episode of *The Golden Girls* stood out. Had no one warned them about the mighty waves, we wondered, the stormy winds, the enormous splashes the whales would make? A young Japanese couple with sophisticated cameras was whispering to each other under a photo of a pack of orca whales. They responded to our greetings with a shy smile. In another corner we met a British family who came to New Zealand with their young kids, a boy and girl.

After half an hour, the company informed us that due to harsh weather conditions, all scheduled sailings were canceled. We were relieved at the news and went promptly back to sleep at our hostel.

The next morning we went back and were sent back to our hostel again. The entire week was spent like this, in a dreamlike trance, waking up in the middle of the night, trudging to the beach to find out that we could not sail, then trudging back to our hostel. We started to learn more about our bold sailing companions, who with a strange sense of weary determination continued to show up every morning, hoping that today would be the day they would see the magnificent sperm whale. We learned that the old ladies had arrived from the northern island to take part in the adventure; the Japanese couple was on their honeymoon; the British family had come to New Zealand for two months.

It is funny how we get used to new situations. Within a few days, we formed a routine. Every afternoon we met at the bar, stayed there through the night, crashed on our beds in the hostel fully clothed, woke up four hours later, drove to the beach, waited until we got disappointing news, then went back to sleep. Wash, rinse, repeat.

On the fifth day we woke up at four a.m. as usual. The whale watch company had warned all of us not to eat before sailing, which seemed like a sensible warning, but that morning we woke up starving. We prepared and ate a majestic breakfast of toast, mozzarella cheese omelets, orange juice, cereal with milk, and fresh kiwi.

When we arrived at the meeting place, the ocean looked the same as usual, with high waves, biting wind, borderline weather. But the cloudy-eyed group that had gathered on the stairs all week was already inside trying on life vests. It had been decided that tours would depart that day; Odelia and I would sail on the second tour of the day. The guides explained that our chances of seeing a sperm whale were not high; the company promised to refund half the cost if we did not see any whales.

We were advised to acquire special bracelets to protect us from seasickness; the bracelet's hexagonal knot should be placed on an acupuncture point on the forearm. We bought the bracelets and swallowed a few ginger pills for good measure, hoping for the best.

Outside, the ocean was waiting for us. The whale watch company's pamphlets had a picture of a giant whale's beautiful tail against the backdrop of a bright, cloudless sky and the town's snowy mountains. But this was not the view that awaited us. The waves were grey, the winds howled furiously, the sky was ominous. We could not even see the office building in the heavy fog, let alone the mountain peaks.

The catamaran, our means of transportation for the coming hours, was stationed on a huge trailer. We waited on the rocky beach as the first cycle of passengers descended to dry land. They were pale, their hair messy, their eyes glassy.

As soon as they disembarked, our group flooded them with questions. "Did you see whales? How many? How was it?"

The passengers nodded tiredly. Yes, they saw three whales.

"Three," everyone whispered, enthused. "Three whales!"

A giant Māori carried down an old lady in a clear state of exhaustion, but the sight did not dampen our excitement. After all, this was not an experience for softies, we told ourselves. We boarded the catamaran in high spirits. The excitement washed over us like a warm wave. We looked at our travel companions fondly, as they were about to share with us a meaningful experience. An ancient loudspeaker at the bow squeaked, then the captain's voice came out like a metallic thunder with a variety of whistles in the background. He proudly announced that his catamaran was equipped with two Rolls-Royce engines, each cranking four hundred horsepower.

We grinned to ourselves. "Who cares about the horsepower?" But our smiles were erased when the captain started the engines. A throaty, animal-like groan busted out, and within minutes we were deep into the ocean, glued to our seats, slicing the waves at a speed of twenty knots, the mad captain reported, screaming through the loudspeaker.

The catamaran galloped wildly over the ocean, climbing up each wave before beating down on the water with an enormous bang. Water splashed all over the deck. Slowly but surely, our brave team started to break down. The first casualty was a skinny young woman on the seat in front of us who'd seemed scared since we boarded the catamaran. Her vomiting spree was thorough. After the fourth bag, we offered her some ginger pills. She swallowed them gratefully. A moment later, she vomited again, looking utterly defeated.

The Japanese woman was hunched forward like she was praying to something or someone that would save her from this hellish trip. Her husband stroked her head, murmuring calming words until he stopped mumbling, grabbed the vomit bag, and threw up with a loud scream. The British family looked like a shapeless lump, all hunched forward, bracing themselves each time the catamaran hit the surface.

The four old ladies were in excellent shape. They examined the splashing waves with interest, shouting with joy whenever they noticed an albatross gliding over the waves. Meanwhile, the crew continued to look for the sperm whale—not an easy task, given that whales can stay underwater for two hours before coming up for air.

The high waves made it impossible to detect the whales by their air jets, so the crew used waterproof microphones that could detect the sounds whales make underwater. We continued our crazy race.

We realized that the giant Māori was our entertainment officer; his job was to tell bad jokes like "Who cannot swim here?" while trying to educate us about the whales. He said that when the hydrophones detect whale sounds, they would sound to us like a sequence of clicks. With a knowing smile, he added that whales could send love songs through the sonar system. He clicked his tongue, making a series of high-pitched sounds meant to imitate a whale in love. No one seemed amused.

He then tried harder to brighten up the gloomy atmosphere that had taken hold of the catamaran, telling us about the rare cases when a sperm whale, instead of rising to the surface peacefully, had jumped up from the depths in a powerful thrust, fifty tons of incomprehensive might. The Māori said he had seen many cases when the whale's entire body was out of the water!

"What's the point of all these stories?" some of us grumbled. "What about the money we paid?"

The Māori shook his head. An eerie silence engulfed us for the next fifteen minutes. Then out of the blue, the old microphone groaned and made the announcement we had all been waiting for: "We have a whale on the surface!"

The mad captain turned off both Rolls-Royce engines. We all rushed to the upper deck with our cameras ready. The ocean was rough, creating an unsteady feeling. We grabbed the rails, staring into the distance, feeling like

Captain Ahab looking for Moby Dick. Suddenly, we saw an enormous black mass about fifty feet away, spraying jets of water into the air. We could not tell if it was a massive barrel, a Russian submarine from the Cold War, or a massive tree trunk from a faraway place.

The giant Māori addressed us urgently. "There isn't much time. Prepare your cameras—he's going to dive back momentarily. There are three pictures you must catch. I'll tell you exactly when to shoot."

The goal was to catch the amazing picture of the whale's tail stretched like a huge fan against the backdrop of the endless ocean. With a sense of great urgency, I focused the camera on the giant black thing. A few minutes passed. The catamaran continued to wobble from side to side. The rhythmical swinging and the fact that my eyes were glued to the camera put me in a kind of hypnotic trance.

A thick veil of fog started to cover the whale. I heard a scream. Someone shook me down. "Quickly!" the Māori shouted in my ear. "He is diving in!" His voice echoed in my ears, overcoming the furious winds. "Now, now, now!"

I took three quick photos in succession, hoping one of them would get the job done. The whale waved his giant tail to the sky and brought it down to the surface in an enormous blow. Before we realized what was happening, the whale dived to the depths of the ocean floor.

We went back to our seats. The two Rolls-Royce engines thundered again. The British family later told us that in the next hour they saw one more whale, a shark, and a pod of dolphins, but we were glued to our vomit bags, switching them fast. Our healthy breakfast was not so healthy after all. At the corner of our eyes we saw the four old ladies glowing with joy, shouting "yah-oh-hoo-ha" every time the catamaran hit a big wave and bounced back with a loud thud.

When we got to shore we saw the new group of passengers waiting, their eyes shining, hands moving about excitedly. It was hard to believe that a few hours before we'd been standing on dry land, young, beautiful, healthy. We promised them that it was once-in-a-lifetime experience. We did not have the guts to tell them the truth.

When we checked the photos we took, all we could see was a foggy ocean. The whale and his magnificent tail were nowhere to be found. Whenever we remember this adventure at sea, a vague sense of seasickness creeps over us, reminding us that some experiences in life are best experienced just once.

CHAPTER NINE

GIANT WAVES IN HAWAII

WITH A DIRECT FLIGHT BETWEEN New Zealand and Hawaii, we landed at Honolulu International Airport with heavy expectations. In contrast to our tropical fantasies of a virginal island with unspoiled beaches, Waikiki turned out to be a busy city filled with shopping malls, chain restaurants, and traffic. Still, amid this hustle and bustle stretched the amazing Waikiki beaches, so beautiful we could stare at the blue and green ocean for hours.

Our hostel was near one of the less crowded beaches of Waikiki. Every afternoon we saw the surfers return from the beach, chests proud, hair wet, walking briskly with their surfboards on their heads. They had the look of those who had made it and were living the dream of every surfer around the world. In the evenings they would sit out on the balcony, smoke, finish a six-pack, listen to music, and share tall tales about their adventures at sea. To us they looked like the embodiment of bravery on earth—until the hostel owner, an experienced surfer himself, told us that the surfers on this beach were beginners.

"Good only for three-foot waves," he said with a dismissive flick of his hand. We stared at him, astonished.

"If you wish to see real waves with real surfers, you must go to the North Shore," he said.

I'd always had a weakness for high waves. They symbolized absolute freedom for me, the possibility of breaking the rules and conventions of life. The next morning, we were en route to the North Shore of Oahu, crammed into a local bus that took forever to get there.

We arrived at a new hostel that afternoon. This one was surrounded by beautiful tropical vegetation, situated on a former banana plantation. The place had an elusive sense of freedom, the carefree life. While Odelia registered us, I found a bench under one of the swaying palm trees. After several minutes, I heard a dull noise from afar, something resembling a distant explosion accompanied by intimidating thunder. The weather was typically Hawaiian: deep blue skies, a handful of clouds, a light warm breeze that felt so good on my face. The hostel's maintenance crew ignored the noise as they went about their work. The thunder continued to roll in an orderly sequence of explosions. I counted six explosions with a one-minute pause between them, then a three-minute break before the distant booms resumed.

I figured there was road work nearby, and we went up to our room. Odelia was tired, practically falling asleep as soon as she placed her head on the blue pillow. I lay down beside her but could not sleep. The faint sound of the explosions was audible even in our closed room. I rose quietly and left the room. Outside, I saw a skinny blond teenager raking leaves indifferently. I asked him if he knew what was creating the noise. He gave me a bored look, shrugged, and said, "It's only the waves, man, only the waves."

"Only the waves?" I repeated his words, trying to make sense of what he was saying. He noticed my confusion.

"You're in luck," he said, smiling for the first time. "We have a major swell. The waves can be up to thirty feet now."

My heart started to beat faster. He saw the look on my face and pointed toward the road beyond the palm trees. I crossed the road, smelling the scent of the ocean, then crossed a wall of dense bushes. The noise became urgent, but nothing prepared me for the wonderful sight in front of me.

I stood on an empty white sand shore looking at a beautiful bay flanked by outcroppings of rocks that extended into the ocean. In front of me there was an enormous wall of water—about the size of a three-story building—roaring, rattling, moving toward me. This was a huge turquoise wave, embedded with a hundred hues of blue. Before I could take in the amazing sight, the enormous wave crashed in a deafening explosion, detonating with fury upon the rocks.

A moment later, I saw another huge wave moving fast toward the shore. You could not see behind it. The horizon disappeared, and with it the entire world beyond this beach. Another enormous wave rushed toward the beach, and time slowed down for me, then accelerated. The show was marvelous. Six giant waves appeared one after the other, followed by an eerie tranquility when the ocean calmed down, looking like the Sea of Galilee in the early morning hours. After a few minutes, a new set of waves began. Nature was revealed to me in its utmost power. I, who grew up on the shores of the tame Mediterranean, stood there with my mouth wide open at the face of an explosive, infinite power.

Years before, I was asked what my favorite type of body of water was. The inquirer was a bearded, sympathetic psychologist administering a personality test I had to take for a job interview.

"High, stormy waves," I answered without blinking.

"The answer to this question indicates the kind of life a person wishes to live," explained the psychologist. "Some choose a calm fountain or a quiet lake. We know they are looking for a steady, predictable life. The ones who choose stormy waves, raging rivers, or steep waterfalls wish to live with lots of ups and downs." For whatever reason, I did not get that job. Perhaps they were looking for a more conservative, even-tempered candidate.

Standing on that white beach, mesmerized by the high waves, I remembered making the decision to move to the United States at the age of twenty-one, transforming the course of my life. Fragments of memories floated around me in the fragrant air, merging with the thick spray from the waves.

I remembered a happy childhood that was cut short when my father became disabled and lost his job. Everything changed for my family afterwards. We desperately tried to keep an air of normalcy with a father who spent as much time in hospital beds as in his own bed. Despite the tornados that repeatedly smashed our naïve hopes that everything would be all right, at the end of the day I came through to the other side. I knew that there was steel in me, the kind that is paid for with harsh life lessons. Although I wished none of that would have happened, that my childhood could have been different, I felt a strange sense of pride in looking into the eye of the storm and surviving it.

The waves continued to roar around me as my head filled with memories. I saw an excited, anxious young man boarding a plane with a one-way ticket to the United States and a suitcase containing clothes and what I thought would be the key to my future in my new country: three thick volumes of a Hebrew-English dictionary. Seven years later I returned to Israel for my father's shiva, the week of mourning before his funeral, that ushered in the momentous arrival of Odelia, who came to offer her condolences and entered my life in the most unexpected way.

I remembered an elaborate marriage proposal in New York City, then the moment we decided to take a trip around the world with no time limit.

The mighty waves rose and fell before me. I smiled. Nothing in my life up to that moment had been routine. My life had unfolded exactly the way it should have.

I stayed at the beach for an hour, taking in the sights and sounds. I was grateful to be given the chance to witness such mighty waves, but I still felt the urge to be closer to them, to see them in their full glory, to be inside them when they broke, to merge with this amazing energy. The best way to merge with the waves was, of course, to try to surf them, but I had no illusions about my ability to do so.

On the left side of the bay a cluster of black rocks sent a long tongue into the ocean. Giant waves were crashing on the rocks, raising clouds of foam and sea spray and roaring in cruel madness. I tried to imagine a path to climb them but couldn't find one. Standing there seemed even more dangerous than surfing. But then I saw a distant figure at the far end of the rocks, awfully close to the breaking waves. It was a young man with long hair and his arms stretched, engulfed in the mist.

If he had dared to climb, I could, too. After a difficult climb on the slippery rocks, I reached the point where the waves were breaking right in front of me. The thunder was deafening, and as I pulled myself up to stand on the cliff's head, a stunning sight opened in front of me. The waves surrounded me. I was inside them, feeling their brutal power from up close. As a massive wave approached me, I examined this beast of nature that stared back with a giant turquoise eye, like a huge predator spotting easy prey that had not correctly estimated its ability to escape imminent danger. The wave closed the distance with frightening speed, and then, at the last minute, crashed at the bottom of the cliff, covering me with a blanket of ocean spray.

The contrast between the waves and the perfect weather was breathtaking. Blue skies, soft wind blowing, warm sun stroking, and silvery mountains of water coming from nowhere, appearing from the horizon, making their way to the shore like a giant snake slithering in the ocean. I stood on the slippery, pointed rocks in the land of the giant waves, counting my blessings.

The waves continued to rise from the depth of the sea in mysterious sets. I felt like I could stand there forever. I had never experienced such a powerful life force. I vibrated with happiness each time a giant wave crashed in front of me, sending a cloud of spray to the sky. For no apparent reason, the waves started to get bigger, more menacing. A huge wave rose in front of me, advancing from the depths of the ocean like an avalanche in the mighty Himalayas, sweeping everything in its way.

This was the biggest wave I had ever seen, a leviathan of the ocean. I looked behind me. It was too late to turn back, to find shelter among the slippery rocks. It was one of those situations in life where you knew that you must stand your ground, face head-on whatever is coming at you. I held on to the rock in front of me, trying to find a grip that would keep me there in case the wave swept over the rocks. My heart was beating at a record speed.

"If I survive this mountain, the Everest of the ocean, I will get back to the shore," I promised myself. I knelt, and from the corner of my eye I saw the other nutcase standing up with his back against the black rock, eyes closed, head leaning backward, arms outstretched. The approaching wave's noise drowned out everything around me. It continued to advance at a speed that increased by the second. I grabbed the rock, the wall of green water upon me, ready to devour me. The noise was deafening and as I closed my eyes, I disappeared in a mighty explosion.

Silence.

I was drenched, but in one piece. The ocean was calm. It seemed that the wave had crashed on the middle of the cliff, not at its base. The rocks around me were covered in water. I heard the young man's scream from afar: "Are you all right?"

I signaled to him that everything was okay.

"This was the greatest wave today!" the lad shouted.

I nodded, still thrilled by the powerful experience. Though I had promised myself that if I survived the monster, I would get off the rock and return to the beach, I stayed on the rocks for another hour. The giant wave never came back, but if I had been lucky enough to encounter another mountain like that, I would have accepted it with arms outstretched, like the young man on the rocks ahead of me.

The waves crashed around me, flooding me with cold sprinkles, the sun warmed my face, and I felt an immense sense of joy.

CHAPTER TEN

THE VAGABONDS

WHEN I WAS TWELVE YEARS old, I watched the movie *Papillon* starring Steve McQueen. It's the story of a French prisoner by the name of Henri Charrière, who was serving a life sentence at Devil's Island, a notoriously brutal prison colony off the coast of French Guiana in South America. The place reeks of desperation, a shark-infested pile of rocks in the middle of the Atlantic Ocean. The last scene of the movie made a great impression on me back then, and even now, when I watch the original movie, it moves me.

Steve McQueen stares at the infinite blue ocean from an enormous cliff on Devil's Island. There are no guards around, as no one has ever escaped from this desolate place. Huge waves break powerfully on the cliff's pointed, lofty walls, roaring like an animal detecting easy prey. Henri, who never gave up on his hope to be a free man, now has white hair. Some of his teeth are missing, and his eyesight is weak from long stays in the dungeon. His only friend, Louis Dega (played by Dustin Hoffman), has accepted the fact that he will die on this lonely cliff in the middle of the ocean, but Henri has a different plan.

After a long period of observation, Henri is convinced they can escape by jumping off the cliff into the ocean, then drifting on jute bags filled with coconuts until they reach shore. He somehow manages to convince his old friend to join him in this last adventure.

They stand together on the mighty cliff, looking down at the raging ocean below, making their final reckoning. The wind blows furiously around them. Henri throws down his bag of coconuts, and the bag makes its long, slow, arcing way to the wild waves. Louis Dega watches the bag's flight, reflecting on the arc of his own life. Even before the bag touches the waves, he understands that he will not be able to join his good friend. The adventure is too big for him. He has come to terms with his fate, and a dramatic jump into the unknown is something that he, like any ordinary person, would never seriously consider.

But Henri Charrière is not an ordinary person. His long years in unbearable conditions, and the cruel penalties he's suffered for every failed escape, have only made him more determined to be a free man. Physically he is a shadow of his former self, a ghost of the healthy, robust man he used to be. But mentally he is ready to make his dream come true. He embraces Louis for the last time, smiles at him with a toothless mouth, then jumps off the cliff.

He floats in the air in a leap that seems to last forever.

When he reaches the water, he disappears in the raging waves—until we see him swimming toward the coconut bag. With enormous effort he manages to swim away from the narrow bay, and as the camera zooms in for a close-up shot, we hear the old man scream, "I'm still here, you bastards!" This is the victory of the human spirit: a heroic, exciting struggle to win back one's freedom.

"Don't mourn me," he says from over the waves. "I'm not dead yet. I will show you that I can get away from you."

We met people with this kind of free-spirit numerous times on our trip, in different countries and continents. They were the real thing, people who had left everything behind to choose wandering as a way of life.

Before we set off on our way, we thought we were quite unique in our decision to sell all our belongings and depart for a carefree trip around the world. Only after a long time on the road did we comprehend what it really means to be a wanderer, not just a backpacker on a specific journey.

At first sight, the wanderer's life seems like the realization of a childhood fantasy. You get to go to exotic locations, view amazing landscapes, meet interesting people, and most importantly, not worry about paying your mortgage, cable, or phone bill. When you become tired of one place, you pack up your few things and move on to the next destination. The wanderer's journey never ends; it goes on forever.

Two of the most memorable wanderers we met on our trip were Dennis and Howard. Like Henri Charrière, they were prepared to pay a steep price for their personal freedom. Their life stories make for great inspiration or head-scratching, depending on your point of view. Both were colorful, interesting characters that were not ready to accept a normal, banal life, and the many ups and downs in their lives revealed the price they had to pay for their unusual choice. Both were highly intelligent; Howard even had a graduate degree from Yale in applied math. They were not hippies, but rather people who made the deliberate, conscious choice to wander the world indefinitely.

We met Dennis in Pokhara, Nepal, in Michael the Boss's restaurant. He was a forty-year-old Canadian who spent his time on the balcony reading the daily English paper while drinking enormous amounts of green tea. He ignored everything around him, but the guests had a hard time ignoring him because he had such an impressive appearance—a brushed-back white mane, piercing blue eyes, and a sturdy body. In short, the look of an important business executive on vacation.

Like all real wanderers, Dennis had no phone number or permanent address anywhere in the world. He told us that he grew up with five brothers but had cut ties with all of them. His relationship with his parents had always been quite loose, and since his mother's death his family had been disconnected. As far as friends, Dennis never talked about them, and we did not dare to press on.

He was like a polar bear who stuffs himself in the summer so that in the winter he can slowly burn fat. When he needed money, he traveled to Australia to pick fruit for a few months, then go on his way. He once showed us a crumpled piece of paper that he always carried with him. The paper listed various crops that are grown in Australia: citrus, pears, mangoes, avocados—and the harvest month for each crop. This piece of paper was Dennis's lifeline. Whenever he felt his finances running low, he would take the paper from his back pocket and plan his next move based on time of the year.

But seasonal work was only one way to keep traveling around the world. A true world citizen, Dennis had seen plenty of places. He had traveled extensively in the Middle East in more touristic countries like Israel, Egypt, and Jordan, and less traveled countries such as Iraq, Syria, Iran, Pakistan, and Afghanistan. He did not brag about his travels but described them in a no-nonsense tone of voice. "The food here reminds me of the Ali Baba restaurant in Baghdad," he once said over a mouthful of beef kebabs, or, "There is a fountain like this in the central square in Damascus."

Dennis had an intimate knowledge of all the places that he had visited, mostly due to a photographic memory coupled with compulsive reading of newspapers. He made it a point to read any French or English paper available in any given place he visited.

"Fourteen percent of Thai citizens are Chinese," he told us when we talked about the situation in Thailand. When we discussed minorities in the United States, he nodded his head, then said, "You know that in thirty years there will be more minorities than white people."

When we realized his phenomenal abilities, we started playing trivia with him. We bombarded him with questions and he answered without missing a beat.

"How many languages do they speak in the Vanuatu islands?"

"A hundred," Dennis said nonchalantly, shaking his head at how easy our question is.

"In what year did Nepal declare its first democratic elections?"

"Nineteen ninety-one," Dennis said indifferently. "I participated in the celebrations in Katmandu."

For every question we asked, Dennis had a detailed, elaborate answer. The problem was that he had no one to share his knowledge with. He moved from one place to the other like an albatross, landing and taking off without leaving a trace—neither feelings nor emotions. His human interactions were limited to a few sentences he shared with a bus driver, a hostel owner, a food seller. He despised pretense, and most travelers seemed like amateur actors to him, bragging about places he knew intimately. He was not impressed with the excited, often exaggerated travel stories of other backpackers, yet he was not keen to talk about his own vagabond way of life.

The big trip that for most people was a once-in-a-life-time experience, the fulfillment of a dream, was a regular way of life for Dennis. His escape from routine had paradoxically become his routine. Despite the absolute alienation he demonstrated towards any specific flag or nationality, deep down he was a proud Canadian patriot. He had mixed feelings about his homeland. He loved the vast landscapes and described them with rare emotion, but he also felt that Canada was closed in, not truly open to the world. He hadn't visited for more than ten years, but when we asked him where he would have lived his life if he had to stay in one place, he answered unequivocally: Canada.

I remember very well a conversation we had with him in the new restaurant I designed for Michael the Boss. The sun was setting and a pleasant breeze blew in from the Pokhara Lake. We were alone with Dennis in the restaurant, talking about our plans, including how many children we would like to have. Dennis scratched his neck while we were talking, clearly uncomfortable with the topic of raising a family. When Odelia asked him if he ever thought about settling down, he admitted, halfheart-edly, that he was afraid of entering into a relationship that would tie him to one place. When we asked if he'd ever wished to have children of his own, he shrugged as if struggling against powerful forces, saying that it wasn't meant for him, that it wasn't in the cards anymore. I thought to myself that even though Dennis was an odd bird, he could have been a wonderful father, someone who could give and receive love.

The second time we met him was in Dharamshala, in northern India. We were looking for a jeep that would take us to the Golden Temple in Amritsar, right on the border with Pakistan, and Dennis responded to a note we placed in a local café asking for travelers who would like to share the cost of the ride with us. When he knocked smartly on the door to our shabby room, I was certain that the Israeli ambassador himself had come to deliver an important message.

But then I recognized our friend, and that knock on our door continued the wonderful friendship that had developed against the backdrop of exotic locations in India, Nepal, Thailand, and Australia. We'd met him in all these places, always incidentally, at various odd spots. I believe that if we hadn't met him so many times, our friendship wouldn't have evolved; Dennis was a lone wolf who had a hard time forming meaningful human contact. His extended journeys around the world had trained him for total independence and raised his protective walls.

We met him for the last time in Sydney, Australia, and spent an entire week together before going our separate ways. We knew it would be the last time we saw him, as we were going to New Zealand and Hawaii while Dennis was heading back to the Far East.

I urged him to give us his phone number or an address where we could leave him messages.

Dennis looked anxious. "What address can I give you?"

"Whichever you like . . ."

"But I'm not sure where I would be—maybe in India, Thailand, Vietnam . . ."

"It makes no difference. Even an address of friends or relatives in Canada."

He didn't say anything.

I added, "So we may keep in touch."

There was a long pause. Dennis stared at me for a second, then mumbled, "Maybe Peter from Canada, we went to high school together."

"No problem." I was happy. "What's Peter's address?"

"Whose?"

"Peter, your Canadian friend."

Dennis searched his worn-out backpack for a thin notebook. He quickly leafed through it.

"I can't find his new address," he said, shaking his head in confusion. "He might have moved somewhere else three years ago."

Eventually we gave him the address of Odelia's parents in Israel.

Dennis accompanied us to the central bus station in Sydney, where we would take the bus to Melbourne. On the way we reminisced about our common experiences. He seemed calm, so we assumed that this farewell, like those preceding it, would be without any display of emotion. When the bus arrived, we collected our back-packs and started to move toward the bus. I put my hand on his shoulder and looked at him.

He had tears in his eyes. Dennis tried to say something, but the words were stuck in his throat. The tears rolled down his cheeks, and he did not try to wipe them off. He embraced us, heaving with emotion, and then released us, turned around, and started to walk away. We wanted to follow him, to tell him we would not forget him, that we would think about him, but the bus was leaving. I looked through the bus window, hoping to see him, but he had disappeared forever.

Since then, we have not heard from him. Chances are, he's still wandering the crowded, steamy streets of Bangkok, Katmandu, or Delhi, a nameless vagabond among millions of poor people who despite unbearable living conditions manage to find some moments of happiness every day. I stopped expecting a letter or a postcard from Dennis, but I still think about him occasionally, hoping that he is finding happiness within his vagabond life.

Our second wanderer was Howard. He had all the characteristics of a real vagabond, a lone wolf who did not make contact easily and had no permanent address or phone number. To top it all off, his past was shrouded in mystery. In contrast to Dennis, Howard was a bona fide intellectual who read complex math books for pleasure and regarded newspapers, movies, and any other form of mass media with deep disdain.

We met him at a youth hostel in Melbourne. He was preparing a strange concoction of vegetable puree, date sauce, coconut milk, and cooked carrots. It looked worse than it sounds. Howard gave off the air of someone who was not looking to start a conversation under any circumstances. He always sat in the far corner of the hostel's dim kitchen, eating his awful dishes, never participating in discussions or conversations.

Howard was about fifty, short, bearded, and scrawny. His sunken eyes darted around nervously, as if afraid to make eye contact. The combination of his twitchy eyes and the thick, black beard that covered his entire face gave him the appearance of a mad hermit. Howard did not care much about fashion; his go-to look included a worn, broad-brimmed hat, khaki shorts that hung upon his skinny, hairy knees, and one of two T-shirts: one that read "Born to Be Free," the other with a large YES printed across the entire shirt. He looked like someone who'd never seen the inside of a library or read a book in his life, but he received his first degree in physics at the age of eighteen, and at twenty earned a graduate degree in applied math from Yale.

His meteoric rise in academia ended when he decided to take a year off to travel across the United States. That one year became years of wandering around the world. For some reason, Howard refused to travel to Third World countries, so he kept moving between the United States, Europe, Australia, and New Zealand. He lived frugally, and when he ran out of money he worked any number of odd jobs. When he told us about his education, I found it hard to believe that this homeless-looking vagabond was some kind of lost genius that happened to be in the same shabby hostel as us, so I decided to test him, pretty much like we did with Dennis.

"Odi," I would ask Odelia in an indifferent tone, knowing that Howard was nearby, "can you please check your calculator? If Australia has 25,000,000 citizens, and it is 7,682,300 square kilometers, how many people are there in one square kilometer?"

"Three point two five," Howard muttered quietly before Odelia had a chance to pull the calculator from her backpack.

Later, we discovered that Howard also had an uncanny ability to read maps. At any given point in our journey, he knew exactly where we were just by a quick glance at the map. When we met him in Melbourne, Australia, we were planning a trip to the Great Ocean Road, an area with wild, beautiful beaches stretching for three hundred miles from Melbourne to Adelaide. After three days of getting to know Howard, he told us that he was planning to travel the Great Ocean Road and invited us to join him in his car. In return, he offered to share the travel expenses.

"My car isn't big," he said, "but it's a station wagon, so there's plenty of room. I think we would feel like one big happy family."

We grabbed the bargain happily, without considering how Howard might define the words "happy" or "family."

We arranged to meet him at the bus station in an old miners' town that was built at the height of the gold rush. He arrived three hours late, heavily panting.

"I saw some nice buildings on the way and stopped for a while to take some photos," he explained with short breath. We figured photography was one of his passions, and ignored this ominous sign.

When we saw our mode of transportation for the next week, our jaws dropped in disbelief. The car was an old Australian creation, similar to a Mini-Minor, that Howard, as if he were the owner of a classic luxury vehicle, kept bragging about. He told us they discontinued this model twenty years ago. It was technically a station wagon, but as Howard lifted the rusty trunk door, we were shocked to see that the car was already filled with all of Howard's belongings on this earth.

We looked at each other, shaking our heads. How the hell could we get into the car with our backpacks? It was like one of those annoying riddles about fitting an elephant into a Volkswagen. Howard's stuff was crammed everywhere: on the front seat, on the tiny back seat, on the gear box, suffocating the back window, filling the small trunk. We tried several times until we had no choice but to take everything out of the car and place all his belongings on the sidewalk. The items piled up and included a battered tent, a dirty sleeping bag, a small inflatable raft, a gas stove, two plates, two knives, a fork and a spoon, a small pot, another small pan, a picnic box, a military surplus coat, a shoebox full of used math books, various cans that seemed as if they were purchased at a clearance sale from a desperate shopkeeper, Howard's backpack, and of course, our own two packs.

Howard suggested that we get into the car first. Then he would hand us the rest of the stuff, piece by piece. We squeezed in. He looked at us, took a mental note of his belongings, and realized he would need to make some hard choices.

"I will sell some of my things, make some money," he informed us in a serious tone. He decided to target the small crowd that had gathered to watch the show. We kept silent. Two hours later, Howard was richer by forty dollars and we were jammed in like refugees escaping an earthquake in the last vehicle available. Howard and I sat up front, separated by the tent. The gear box was on my side, so we developed an original driving system in which Howard would step on the clutch while shouting, "First gear now, shift to second," or "shift down to third," and I would move the gears accordingly.

Odelia was in the back, barely visible. Getting in and out of the car meant organizing the luggage anew, which took ten minutes every time. If it was a normal drive in which one stopped once or twice to freshen up, so be it! But the drive with Howard was far from normal. The Great Ocean Road between Melbourne and Adelaide winds along astonishing beaches of lime rocks that look as if they were designed by an artist, sculptures stationed in the wild ocean. The road is rightfully considered one of the most beautiful in the world.

Our trouble began when we saw the sign that changed our experience from exciting to nightmarish: SCENIC OUTLOOK.

"I have to see what it is," our driver called, turning toward the sign. Once we arrived, we spent ten minutes getting out of the car to get to the observation post. In the distance was a glimmer of the vast ocean that surrounds Australia. Howard took careful photos, pondering the view with a serious look. Thirty minutes later we squeezed in all our stuff and resumed our drive.

After about fifteen minutes, another sign announcing a scenic outlook appeared on the side of the road. We stopped again, unloaded our equipment, watched Howard take pictures, reloaded the luggage. This happened at regular intervals on the first day. Howard insisted on stopping at each observation post, anxious that he would miss a viewpoint that he had not seen before. To us, all these viewpoints seemed the same. By early afternoon, we'd stopped at fifteen observation posts. With practice, our time of getting in and out of the car improved; by lunchtime we were able to shave two full minutes from the process, a record we were proud of.

Since Howard was in constant fear of missing out, he had the annoying habit of turning onto unmarked dirt roads to see if there was something interesting at the end of the road. Australia is a vast country; one cannot foretell if the road that you've turned onto will bring you to a scenic spot or meander on endlessly. Sometimes we jolted along a no-man's path for an hour or more until Howard gave up and turned back.

By the end of the first day, we'd spent fourteen hours in the car and only managed to advance fifteen miles. At midnight, utterly exhausted, we stopped in a small town for the night. Odelia and I were beat from the crazy day, but Howard declared that he was going to tour the town. Early the next morning, he woke us up to continue this nightmarish trip.

This routine went on for a whole week. Our trip became a kind of weird, surreal experience. We would wake up, pack everything in the tiny car, stop multiple times along the way for scenic lookouts, travel along unmarked dirt roads that led nowhere for hours, and get to a hostel around midnight. Howard was a stern taskmaster with no appetite for human connection. He insisted on leaving our hostels first thing in the morning, before anyone else got up.

He was also obsessed with the end of humanity on earth due to pollution and waste and would deliver scary apocalyptic speeches. To make his point, he walked around with garbage bags and collected any trash that he came upon. If he realized that a hostel was not keen on recycling, he got over his aversion for human contact, looked for the owner, then presented a series of somber end-of-the-world scenarios.

He hated television shows of any kind, which represented to him a sinister plot by cynical politicians and global corporations to control the minds of the population. Television symbolized for Howard the sad state of humanity, a victory of stupidity over deep thinking. Whenever we were in a hostel with a television on, he tried turning it off or muting the sound. One evening we forced him to watch *Indiana Jones and the Raiders of the Lost Ark*; Howard sat as if he had been forced by the devil, holding a complicated math book to protect himself from the Hollywood brainwash. He did not look in his book even once during the movie, but would not let us be pleased for a moment when he summed up the movie as "a total waste of cinematic talent."

After a week of traveling with Howard and advancing only a fifth of the way from Melbourne to Adelaide, we decided to part ways with this nut-head and get on a bus to Adelaide. To this day, when we see a sign announcing a scenic spot, we accelerate.

Our encounters with Dennis and Howard proved to us how far we were from being real vagabonds. On one hand, we began to understand why real wanderers seemed indifferent to their whereabouts. The energy we felt at the beginning of the trip dissipated. The first time we saw an elevated lake in the Himalayas, we spent an entire morning photographing it from all angles. Less than a year later when we saw another such lake in the New Zealand Alps, we didn't even bother to stop the car.

Unlike Howard and Dennis, when the trip became routine, we got fed up with it. We did not wish to make it a way of life. We yearned for a place of our own, somewhere we could unpack our backpacks for a long time. We missed home-cooked food. A good conversation with friends. Our families. We did not want to become nameless vagabonds. We wished to belong. We wanted to go on with our lives.

We also knew that life would not be the same to us anymore. We'd managed to fulfill our dream. We went to places we'd wished to see. We met people we would never forget. We became acquainted with faraway places and strange cultures, getting a better feel for what makes us feel alive.

The trip also deepened our understanding of each other. We learned to trust one another, and the experiences we shared provided a solid foundation for our future. Maybe that was the trip's greatest contribution: that we came to know we could do something extraordinary with our lives. We can break the routine and reroute the river of life from the familiar, clear path it usually flows in.

It's said that if you want to understand someone, you should walk a mile in their shoes. We had walked quite a distance in vagabonds' shoes, learning about their point of view. We gathered that even if we wanted to, we'd never be real wanderers.

We knew it was time to sign off on this chapter in our lives and begin a new one: that of children, a mortgage, and all other kinds of responsibilities. Whenever we remember Deepak, Doug, Muhammad, Howard, Dennis, the Tessring family, Shimon, and Keren—and of course, when we remember the greatest of all, Michael the Boss—we smile, feeling deeply grateful for all these experiences. We fulfilled our dream.

As the years passed after our grand tour, our children, Maya, Jonathan, and Daniel, began to join us on adventures in Peru, Mexico, Japan, and Costa Rica. Granted, these trips are shorter, more intense versions of the year we spent backpacking around the world. The pace is different, but the opportunity to immerse in a culture and make new friends in faraway places is as exciting as meeting Noshad the crazy driver or Doug from Broken Hill.

When we left for that first trip, one of our close friends said we were taking a year-long break from real life. I strongly disagree. In that year, I felt more alive than in many of the years that followed. Life is not meant for chasing whatever everyone else around us is pursuing. We realized the real meaning of life is to grab your dreams by the horn, hold tight, and make a go for it without any regrets. At the end of the day, what else can you ask for than a life with minimal regrets?

I wish that sense of conviction, of absolutely knowing that *this* is what I need to do, could accompany me in all areas of life. But life is unpredictable. It is tough to make decisions when presented with so many options. I hope if this feeling of certainty finds me again, it will lead to another great adventure. I know it would be a decision I would not regret.

The End

ACKNOWLEDGMENTS

THIS BOOK COULDN'T HAVE BEEN completed without the encouragement and support of my family. My wife Odelia, the co-pilot on this amazing journey, kept a daily diary during our trip around the world. Even though I often questioned the usefulness of writing down everything that happened to us, her diary proved indispensable when it came to writing this book.

My daughter Maya kept asking when the book will be completed, pushing me in the right direction. My son Jonathan read the manuscript and offered useful suggestions, and my youngest son Daniel provided valuable feedback and helped with the cover design.

My parents, Joseph and Joheved, showed me from an early age what it means to be a world traveler. Keter Publishing House, and especially Danny Dor, the editor-in-chief, saw the potential of the book and offered to publish it in Israel.

Dalia Gal took the unenviable task of translating the book from Hebrew to English, creating a faithful and spirited translation. Meghan Pinson did a splendid job with copy editing. David Wogahn, my publishing consultant, helped in every step of the way, from cover design to formatting to invaluable guidance on the publishing industry. I couldn't have done it without him.

Finally, to all my beta readers who provided timely and insightful comments on the text. I deeply appreciate your time, effort, and commitment.

ABOUT THE AUTHOR

EYAL DANON IS THE AUTHOR behind *Before the Kids and Mortgage*. This book was originally published in Israel by Keter Publishing House, after winning a national competition for the best travel story. Eyal is a Columbia University-trained life coach, and the founder of Ignite Advisory Group, a global leader in managing expert communities.

His upcoming books include *The Golden Key of Gangotri*, an exciting novel about a father lost in ice, secrets shrouded by time, and a perilous expedition into the source of the holy Ganges river, and *The Principle of 18*, an innovative self-help system for getting the most out of every stage of your life by fulfilling the promise of five distinct life chapters.

Eyal lives in New Jersey with his family, trying to embrace the four seasons of the Northeast after growing up surfing the Mediterranean Sea. He enjoys reading anything by J.R.R. Tolkien, hiking, table tennis, and Japanese whiskey.

Connect with Eyal on www.eyaldanon.com.

CPSIA information can be obtained
at www.ICGtesting.com
Printed in the USA
BVHW081658220321
603177BV00004B/124

9 781736 299401